# The Alpha and The Omega of Apostasy

By
Julius Gilbert White

**TEACH Services, Inc.**
P U B L I S H I N G
www.TEACHServices.com • (800) 367-1844

Copyright © 2005 TEACH Services, Inc.
ISBN-13: 978-1-57258-305-4 (Paperback)
Library of Congress Control Number: 20040999422

**TEACH Services, Inc.**
PUBLISHING
www.TEACHServices.com ● (800) 367-1844

# Introduction

Ellen G. White, in *Testimonies*, Series B, No. 2, p. 16, wrote the following: "Be not deceived; many will depart from the faith, giving heed to seducing spirits and doctrines of devils. We have now before us the alpha of this danger. The omega will be of a most startling nature."

Julius Gilbert White (1878–1955) well understood this message, he could clearly see what the *alpha* of apostasy was and what the omega would be, and he also understood the dangers involved. After much research and study the author put together a manuscript which he originally entitled *Apostasy Among Seventh-day Adventists-The Alpha and the Omega, The Nature of Our Disease*, which, unfortunately, has never been published before, the reason being unknown.

It is believed that the author wrote this manuscript in the latter part of his life. Many years have passed by since, and in September of 1986 a copy of the manuscript was presented to us; we read it through, and found its message to be very timely and very much applicable to all Adventists who are waiting for the soon coming of our Lord Jesus Christ. Helped by some believers, we have made the necessary efforts to make this work available to all sincere Adventists who want to know the truths for our time.

In this work the reader will find a message that is easy to understand, and it is our hope that the materials found in it will be of great value to all who open its pages with the purpose of wanting to know more of God's holy will.

# Contents

# Apostasy

A great deal is being said in various quarters about apostasy among us. Probably not as much is being said as ought to be, and most likely the right thing is not always said. However, people usually sadly admit that in spirituality we as a people in the United States are steadily declining and growing more worldly, and getting farther and farther from the "latter rain" every day. Facts and statistics and statements could be given to show this, but it is hardly necessary. It is one of the first things every returning foreign missionary discovers.

There are disaffected factions in various places (and being represented nearly everywhere in one way or another) who have plans for reforming the denomination. There are also those within the organization talking about reformation. Various kinds of diagnoses of our condition are made by those factions and also by those within the organization in good and regular standing.

Reformation is most certainly the thing we need, but we need a reformation of the right kind. God has said that we would be handicapped by various kinds of false reformations.

"I saw that God has honest children among the nominal Adventists and the fallen churches, and before the plagues shall be poured out, ministers and people will be called out from these churches and will gladly receive the truth. Satan knows this; and before the loud cry of the third angel is given, he raises an excitement in these religious bodies, that those who have rejected the truth may think that God is with them. He hopes to deceive the honest and lead them to think that God is still working for the churches. But the light will shine, and all who are honest will leave the fallen churches and take their stand with the remnant." —*Early Writings, p. 261.*

It behooves us to know our condition—the origin and cause and nature of our apostasy (have a correct diagnosis)—or we will be sure to apply a wrong reformation (remedy), if we apply any at all.

It is the hope of the writer that the study of a few statements from the Spirit of Prophecy on this subject will shed definite light upon the present situation.

To introduce the matter and get a sure foothold in some definite spot as a beginning place (like driving a stake to which we can tie and from which we can feel out in various directions), we quote the following, written December 4, 1905:

"One thing it is certain is soon to be realized—the great apostasy, which is developing and increasing and waxing stronger, and will continue to do so until the Lord shall descend from heaven with a shout....If we needed the manifest proof of the Holy Spirit's power to confirm truth in the beginning, after the passing of the time, we need today all the evidence in the confirmation of the truth, when souls are departing from the faith and giving heed to seducing spirits and doctrines of devils." —*Testimonies, Series B, No. 7, p. 57.*

The points to be noted carefully here are that the apostasy mentioned in 1905 would increase till the end, and there would be continual departure from the faith and heed given to seducing spirits and doctrines of devils.

The following statement seems to indicate that this would come to a head or crisis after the death of Sister White:

"Great things shall come to pass after I am gone; Satan will work as never before. All that can be shaken will be shaken out. We must draw near to God, for we cannot lean upon man or the crowd. We must know the Lord deeply as never before." —*Mrs. E. G. White, Reported by letter by W. C. White to Far Eastern Division May 1915, and printed in Asiatic Division News May 1-15, 1915, p. 43.*

According to this, a terrible shaking was to come to us after 1915, something far worse than anything preceding it in our denominational history.

"False theories will be mingled with every phase of experience, and advocated with Satanic earnestness in order to captivate the mind of every soul who is not rooted and grounded in a full knowledge of the sacred principles of the Word. In the very midst of us will arise false teachers, giving heed to seducing spirits whose doctrines are of Satanic origin. These teachers will draw away disciples after themselves. Creeping in unawares, they will use flattering words, and make skillful misrepresentations with seductive tact." —*Special Testimonies, August 27, 1903 (Unpublished so far as I know).*

From this we see that it was stated in 1903 that false teachers were to arise "in the very midst of us," giving heed to seducing spirits, and that false theories would be mingled with every phase of experience.

## *Alpha and Omega*

Referring again to the days and experiences of 1904 it is written:

"Be not deceived; many will depart from the faith giving heed to seducing spirits and doctrines of devils. We have now before us the alpha of this danger. The omega will be of a most startling nature." —*Testimonies, Series B, No. 2, p. 16, written July 24, 1904.*

This shows plainly that an apostasy had then begun of which the *alpha* was but one part or phase or feature, and that a later development of the same apostasy would be called the *omega* and would be of a most startling nature.

To know exactly what part of the apostasy God meant when He said *alpha*, note the following, written of the book known as *Living Temple*:

"*Living Temple* contains the alpha of these theories. I knew that the omega would follow in a little while; and I trembled for our people."[1] —*Testimonies, Series B, No. 2, p. 53.*

Note in this last quotation she says she trembled for our people because of the *omega*, which indicates the *omega* would attack the entire denomination and so endanger the people.

The changes these theories were to bring about in our work were called a "reformation" (*Ibid., p. 54*). In the reference here given an extended statement is made of what the consequences to our work would be were this so-called "reformation" to continue, and

---

[1] For material on the subject of *Living Temple* and the theories and dangers pointed out, see *Testimonies*, Series B, No. 2 and No. 7, and *Testimonies*, Vol. 8, pp. 255, 335.

among many other statements made are the following:

"Were this reformation to take place, what would result?...Our religion would be changed....Books of a new order would be written." —*Ibid., pp. 54, 55.*

Of course any apostasy, to be effective, must affect our religion and mold the literature of the denomination, whether it be the *alpha* or the *omega*. Note this point, for of this we will speak again later.

The "books of a new order" that would have been written had the *alpha* continued would lead into the error of unduly exalting the physical, the natural, and nature—deifying nature—and minimizing spiritual truth and God.

"The leaders would teach that virtue is better than vice, but, God being removed, they would place their dependence on human power, which, without God, is worthless." —*Ibid., p. 55.*

The thought in this quotation is to be carefully noted, as use will be made of it later.

The *omega* "would soon follow" and would be "of a most startling nature." Naturally it would not startle those who were in it any more than these who were in the *alpha* were startled by it; but those who discerned it would be greatly startled by it.

The *alpha* grew up in and involved a department or section of the denomination in a special and particular way. But this was not all; the body also was affected by it, and was given a "bent" from which it has not recovered to this day. Evidence of this is in the fact that in some measure or form the alienation then and thereby created between the medical part of the work and the other parts of it has never been healed. From that day to this an unseen hand has made constant attempts to drive wedges between these two parts, to keep them both alienated and both crippled, while God has sent many messages calling for the union of these two and outlining the basis of unity. Herein is a point to be considered most carefully and seriously.

At that time the denomination as a body braced itself against error to reject it and safeguard itself against it. While bracing against the errors in the medical work, it also to a certain extent braced itself against the truths of the medical work; for, beyond all question or doubt, God committed a wonderful message to the medical workers and called them to do a marvelous work. After the separation the truths for which the medical workers had stood were more or less discredited and repudiated along with the errors; and this same process has also continued to this day.

Just to cite a bit of evidence that such were the steps taken, we quote:

"God does not endorse the efforts put forth by different ones to make the work of Dr. Kellogg as hard as possible, in order to build themselves up. God gave the light on health reform, and those who rejected it rejected God. One and another who knew better said that it all came from Dr. Kellogg [the same is said to this day], and they made war upon him. This had a bad influence on the doctor. He put on the coat of irritation and retaliation. God did not want him to stand in a position of warfare, and He does not want you to stand there....God worked through Dr. Kellogg; but men did not realize this....We have the authority of the Bible for our instruction in temperance." —*Testimonies, Series B, No. 6, p. 31.*

This is but a sample of much instruction which has come to us calling the ministry and the body to accept

of health reform and to do medical missionary work
as an important part of the work of the gospel.

# Unity or Division

It seems that God has been standing in the middle between physicians and preachers who have left each other in opposite directions. In thus separating both have left God, and He is reproving both; and when they harmonize again they will both abandon certain ideas which they hold, and both will return to the middle of the road.

We do not mean by this that our physicians have from that time to this been holding and teaching the theories advocated in *Living Temple*, but we do mean that the situation we have now, although it is different from that situation, developed out of that situation.

From that time till now a spiritual viewpoint of the health work has been sadly lacking and with it has continued a lack of close sympathy with the ministry; these things have been inherited from the *alpha*. And furthermore, our health workers have to a deplorable extent departed from the reform elements of the health message; but this will be discussed later in this thesis. These things have all contributed to the continuance of the separation.

On the point of alienation which came in at that time we quote:

"He [Doctor Kellogg] is doing all in his power to create a division between the medical work and the ministry of the word." —*Testimonies, Series B, No. 7,* p. 61.

"Unless there is a breaking away from the influence that Satan has prepared, and a reviving of the testimonies that God has given, souls will perish in their delusion. They will accept fallacy after fallacy, and will thus keep up a disunion that will always exist until those who have been deceived take their stand on the right platform." —*Ibid., p. 63.*

"For years our physicians have been trained to think that they must not give expression to sentiments that differ from those of their chief." —*Testimonies, Series B, No. 2, p. 14.*

From that day to this God has pounded in our ears statements like the following calling for unity:

"The Holy Spirit never has and never will, in the future, divorce the medical missionary work from the gospel ministry. They cannot be divorced. Bound up with Jesus Christ, the ministry of the word and the healing of the sick are one." —*Ibid., No. 7, p. 64.*

These statements show that the seat of the alienation was in theories and sentiments. These differences of teaching separated them from the body, and constituted a cause leading to a desire for an organic separation.

Neither the *alpha* nor the *omega* is primarily an organization of medical folks. The root of an apostasy is not in an association of men but in theology, doctrine, religion, and Christian experience.

When Satan saw the body leaning away from the *alpha*, he saw an opportunity to push the entire body in the direction they were leaning and so unbalanced the entire body; and he went after it.

His plan was to get the theology of the body to be as devoid of the true setting of the physical truth in the spiritual as the *alpha* had been devoid of the true relation of the spiritual to the physical, and so swing the denomination as far away from the physical truths as Kellogg had gone from the spiritual truths. In other words, the medical workers had placed an undue emphasis upon nature and had made it more sacred than it was —had made god of it —and in so doing had really eliminated spiritual truth. Now in repudiating this error it was very easy to conclude that there was no sacredness attached to nature; and in swinging too far in this direction the body joined in the apostasy, but in the opposite or contrary side of it; and when this thing should progress to the point that it has generally affected the theology and Christian experience of the body, then it would rightfully be called the *omega* of the apostasy.

To show that God has for years tried to hold the denomination in the middle between these two extremes, we quote a sample utterance:

"I have been instructed to say, in reference to the medical missionary work, that there is danger of swaying things too heavily in one line. But what I say on this point must not be understood as in any sense justifying those who have held themselves aloof from medical missionary work. There are many who have not been in sympathy with this work. They should now be very careful how they speak in regard to it, for they are not intelligent on the subject because they have not walked in the light. Whatever their position in the work of God, they should be very careful not to give utterance to sentiments that will discourage and hinder our conferences from taking hold of this work. The position that some have occupied in reference to medical missionary work makes it impossible for their words on this subject to have any weight. They are not clear-sighted; their judgment is warped." —*Testimonies, Vol. 8, p. 166.*

In the *alpha* the health work was so prominent that God issued warnings cautioning against making it the whole thing, and:

"Again and again I have been instructed that the medical missionary work is to bear the same relation to the work of the third angel's message that the arm and hand bear to the body. Under the direction of the divine Head they are to work unitedly in preparing the way for the coming of Christ. The right arm of the body of truth is to be constantly active, constantly at work, and God will strengthen it. But it is not to be made the body." —*Ibid., Vol. 6, p. 288.*

As in the *alpha* spiritual truths were to be eliminated, so in the *omega* the health message would be eliminated from the realm of sacred things and become only a tool by which to lead men and women into the realm of sacred things. Thus it would come about that men would not consent that the violation of natural or physical law is sin.

Health would be health, and religion would be religion. The two would be divorced the one from the other. This thought has developed more and more until the great majority of the ministry of the denomination hold this view; and so the theology and religion of the denomination has for years been given this mold, and, note, there has been a corresponding decadence of health reform as given by the Spirit of God, until the abandon to appetite in eating and drinking on the part of our preachers has become proverbial and a byword. Along with this decadence of health reform there has been a corresponding decline in spirituality. That these two must so link together is made plain in the following statement:

"There has been a continual backsliding in health reform, and as a result God is dishonored by a great lack of spirituality." —*Review and Herald, May 27, 1902.*

The Spirit of Prophecy also clearly states the constructive side of this same spiritual condition and shows how this lost spirituality may be regained. Note these two quotations:

"To my ministering brethren I would say,...Combine the medical missionary work with the proclamation of the third angel's message. Make regular, organized efforts to lift the churches out of the dead level into which they have fallen, and have remained for years. Send into the churches workers who will set the principles of health reform in their connection with the third angel's message, before every family and individual. Encourage all to take a part in work for their fellowmen, and see if the breath of life will not quickly return to these churches." —*Special Testimonies for Ministers and Workers, No. 11, 1898, pp. 18, 19.*

"Make regular, organized efforts to lift the church members out of the dead level in which they have been for years. Send out into the churches workers who will live the principles of health reform. Let those be sent who can see the necessity of self-denial in appetite, or they will be a snare to the church. See if the breath of life will not then come into our churches. A new element needs to be brought into the work." —*Testimonies, Vol. 6, p. 267,*

Thus it is clear that our position in these matters constitutes an apostasy away from God and from His living voice in the remnant church.

Therefore, the "gospel of health" has ceased to be a "gospel" because it is said not to be a sin to violate the laws of the body. Having thus eliminated the sacredness of the physical and the sacred duty of obedience to God in the physical realm, the relation of such obedience to Christian experience and character building has become obscured.

And so it has come to pass under the *omega* that "our religion would be changed" and "books of a new order would be written."

Let us now follow through to the conclusion of these things and see how they affect certain great fundamentals, and let us watch to see how insidious they are in their operation—how great is the iniquity wrought and yet how little they apparently change the great fundamentals while in fact entirely undermining them.

In this connection let us ponder the following quotation before proceeding to the study of the things mentioned in the last foregoing paragraph.

"The track of truth lies close beside the track of error, and both tracks may seem to be one to minds not worked by the Holy Spirit, and which, therefore, are not quick to discern the difference between truth and error." —*Testimonies, Series B, No. 2, p. 52.*

When the effect upon Christian experience and character building, which obedience to God in the physical realm produces, is ignored, the field is entered which has to do with:

*Surrender—Faith*

*Prayer—The Holy Spirit*

*The Victorious Life*

*The Latter Rain*

Many of these, and often all of them, are given another and very different setting and interpretation; their relation to Christian experience is altered, and so, to say the least, confusion concerning these and concerning Christian experience is the consequence, and instead of spirituality growing, it wanes, and discouragement and worldliness follow.

Let us illustrate each of these points to make them clear.

## Surrender

"There seems to be in them a heart of unbelief, and, as this reform restricts the lustful appetite, many shrink back. They have other gods before the Lord. Their taste, their appetite is their god; and when the axe is laid at the root of the tree, and those who have indulged their depraved appetites at the expense of health are touched, their sin pointed out, their idols shown them, they do not wish to be convinced; and, although God's voice should speak directly to them to put away those health-destroying indulgences, some would still cling to the hurtful things which they love. They seem joined to their idols and God will soon say to His angels: Let them alone." —*Testimonies, Vol. 1, p. 486.*

This one quotation, from among many that might be given, is sufficient to show that perfect surrender to God cannot be taught and practiced while holding to the views mentioned. These unsurrendered "gods" are of such serious consequence that God will soon say to His angels, Let those people alone. If I will not do what God commands, I have not faith in Him.

## *Faith and Works*

*—Relation Between Is Upset*

The correct relation between faith and works is set forth in these three quotations:

"Let no one listen to the suggestion that we can exercise faith and have all our infirmities removed, and that there is therefore no need of institutions for the recovery of health. Faith and works are not dissevered." —*Testimonies, Vol. 6, p. 441.*

"The health reform, I was shown, is a part of the third angel's message and is just as closely connected with it as are the arm and hand with the human body. I saw that we as a people must make an advance move in this great work. Ministers and people must act in concert. God's people are not prepared for the loud cry of the third angel. They have a work to do for themselves which they should not leave for God to do for them. He has left this work for them to do...one cannot do it for another." —*Ibid., Vol. 1, p. 486.*

"Brethren, we are far behind. Many of the things which the church should do in order to be a living church are not done. Through the indulgence of perverted appetite many place themselves in such a condition of health that there is a constant warring against the soul's highest interests. The truth, though presented in clear lines, is not accepted. I wish to set this matter before every member of our churches. Our habit must be brought into conformity to the will of God. We are assured, 'It is God which worketh in you,' but man must do his part in controlling appetite and passion. The religious life requires the action of mind and heart in harmony with the divine forces. No man can of himself work out his own salvation, and God cannot do this work for him without his cooperation. But when man works earnestly, God works with him, giving him power to become a son of God." —*Testimonies, Vol. 6, pp. 371, 372.*

To illustrate the departure from this, note that one of our noted evangelists speaking at the recent General Conference on the victorious life and overcoming impatience, said, "The doctor tells you that you are weak and nervous and run down and cannot stand as much as some folks. What a liar the devil is!"

This leads to trying to get the victory over impatience by a "faith" that ignores a possible (and likely) physical and mental condition brought on by physical trangression, like diet, overwork, worry, etc.

And having taken this view of the relation between faith and works where matters of health have touched the question and becomes so common here, it most naturally follows that the same view of faith and works is taken in general matters.

And so, faith becomes perverted into presumption, presuming God will do for us that which He commands us to do. But true faith in Him accepts His commands and obeys them. Notice how close together lie the "track of truth and the track of error" before mentioned.

In this connection the following statement concerning Seventh-day Adventist ministers is very significant: "...few ministers know what simple faith is." —*Ibid., Vol. 5, p. 159.*

The true relation between faith and works is again set forth as follows:

"If we are faithful in doing our part, in cooperating with Him, God will work through us to do the good pleasure of His will. But He cannot work through us if we make no effort. If we gain eternal life we must work, and work earnestly....The characters we form here will decide our eternal destiny....Our part is to put away sin, seek with determination for perfection of character. As we thus work, God cooperates with us, fitting us for a place in His kingdom....The doing of God's will is essential if we would have an increased knowledge of Him. Let us not be deceived by the oft-repeated assertion, 'all we have to do is believe.' Faith and works are two oars which we must use equally if we would press our way up the stream against the current of unbelief. 'Faith, if it hath not works, is dead, being alone.' The Christian is a man of thought and practice. His faith fixes its roots firmly in Christ. By faith and good works he keeps his spirituality strong and healthy, and his spiritual strength increases as he strives to work the works of God." —*Review and Herald, June 11, 1901.*

"The faith mentioned in God's word calls for a life in which faith in Christ is an active, living principle. It is God's will that faith in Christ shall be made perfect by works; He connects the salvation and eternal life of those who believe, with these works, and through them provides for the light of truth to go to all countries and peoples. This is the fruit of the workings of God's Spirit.

"We show our faith in God by obeying His commands. Faith is always expressed in words and actions. It produces practical results; for it is a vital element in the life. The life that is molded by faith develops a determination to advance, to go forward, following in the footsteps of Christ." —*Ibid., March 17, 1910.*

"The Salvation of the soul requires the blending of the divine and human strength. God does not propose to do the work that man can do to meet the standard of righteousness. Man has a part to act. Humanity must unite and cooperate with divinity. Grace and sufficiency have been abundantly provided for every soul. But in order to receive this, man must unite with his divine helper. Unless of his own accord man consented to denounce his sinful practices, Christ cannot take away his sin. Man must heartily cooperate with God, willingly obey His laws, showing that he appreciates the great gift of grace. Feeling his dependence upon God, having faith in Christ as his personal Saviour, expecting sufficiency and success only as he keeps the Lord ever before him —it is thus that man complies with the injunction, 'work out your own salvation with fear and trembling.' Human effort is not sufficient. It avails nothing without divine power." —*Signs of the Times, September 25, 1901.*

"True success in any line of work is not the result of chance or accident or destiny. It is the outworking of God's providences, the reward of faith and discretion, of virtue and perseverance. Fine mental qualities and a high moral tone are not the result of accident. God gives opportunities; success depends upon the use made of them.

"While God was working in Daniel and his companions 'to will and to do of His good pleasure,' they were working out their own salvation. (*Philippians 2:13*). Herein is revealed the outworking of the divine principle of cooperation, without which no true success can be attained. Human effort avails nothing without divine power; and without human endeavor, divine effort is with many of no avail. To make God's grace our own, we must act our part. His grace is given to work in us to will and to do, but never as substitute for our effort." —*Prophets and Kings, pp. 486-487.*

## Prayer

Under this perverted Christian experience which we are describing, prayer becomes perverted into an instrument or an endeavor to get something from God against His will rather than a means of bringing man into full harmony with His will. This should be pondered in the light of what has been said about faith and works.

## The Victorious Life

There has been much confusion concerning what the victorious life is and how to achieve it, and as a result false experiences are offered the people.

### —Instantaneous Experience

The false view of faith to which we have referred does not give sufficient room to the experience known as growth or development of the strength of character, and has tended to make the victorious life into a sort of instantaneous experience. For correct teaching on this point note the following quotations:

"Perfection of character is a lifelong work, unattainable by those who are not willing to strive for it in God's appointed way, by slow and toilsome steps. We cannot afford to make any mistake in this matter, but we want day by day to be growing up into Christ our living Head." —Testimonies, Vol. 5, p. 500.

"There is no such thing as instantaneous sanctification. True sanctification is a daily work, continuing as long as life shall last." —Mrs. E. G. White in pamphlet Bible Sanctification, p. 10, published in 1882.

"Sanctification is not the work of a moment, an hour, a day, but of a lifetime. It is not gained by a happy flight of feeling, but is the result of constantly dying to sin and constantly living for Christ. Wrongs cannot be righted nor reformations wrought in the character by feeble, intermittent efforts. It is only by long, persevering effort, sore discipline and stern conflict that we shall overcome. We know not one day how strong will be our conflict the next. So long as Satan reigns, we shall have self to subdue, besetting sins to overcome; so long as life shall last, there will be no stopping place, no point which we can reach and say, I have fully attained. Sanctification is the result of lifelong obedience." —*Acts of the Apostles, pp. 560—561.*

*—A Passive Experience*

The false view of faith also leads to what might be called seeking after the victorious life by a "passive" experience instead of a constant warfare. On this point note the following quotation:

"But Christ has given us no assurance that to attain perfection of character is an easy matter. A noble, all-round character is not inherited. It does not come to us by accident. A noble character is earned by individual effort through the merits and grace of Christ. God gives the talents, the powers of the mind; we form the character. It is formed by hard, stern battles with self. Conflict after conflict must be waged against hereditary tendencies. We shall have to criticize ourselves closely, and allow not one unfavorable trait to remain uncorrected." —*Christ's Object Lessons, p. 331.*

"Let no one imagine that it is an easy thing to overcome the enemy and that he can be borne aloft to an incorruptible inheritance without effort on his part. To look back is to grow dizzy; to let go the hold is to perish. Few appreciate the importance of striving constantly to overcome. They relax their diligence and, as a result, become selfish and selfindulgent. Spiritual vigilance is not thought to be essential. Earnestness in human effort is not brought into the Christian life." —*Testimonies, Vol. 5, pp. 539,540.*

And yet, a certain noted evangelist taught at the late General Conference session: "Victory comes altogether the same as forgiveness....The Christian life is letting Christ do the whole thing"; and this is fairly typical of the general trend of a great deal of the preaching we hear and the articles we read on this subject nowadays in our own ranks. This is not very far removed from the popular teaching of some other Protestant denominations to the effect that we do not have to keep the law because Christ kept it for us, which practically results in assuming an indulgence to sin. Such a substitute of the genuine righteousness of Christ by faith, taken from the confusion of Protestant religion, might appropriately be styled "a Babylonish garment."

*—Conversion*

But you ask, Is not character a thing that is begotten of God by the miracle of the "New Birth"?

Yes, in this sense. This is the time at conversion when the heart has been touched by the Spirit of God and a demand made upon it to surrender. And this is the time when God has presented another viewpoint to the mind, which viewpoint covers everything in the life; this is the time when He presents to us the change in the nature of the heart and offers to give a new heart; "...true conversion is a change of heart, of thoughts and purposes." —*Testimonies, Vol. 6,13. 95.* And this is the time when the decision has been made to change the entire course of the life and begin to perfect the character.

This experience of conversion must be a daily experience ever after as the basis or bottom or foundation of all other experience. This is what is meant in 1 Corinthians 15:31: "I die daily." This is the beginning of the experience and is also to be the beginning of every day's experience, and all the rest is to be builded upon this as a foundation.

After one has submitted the will and the life to God in a thorough consecration to serve Him, there follows a development of the character or a strengthening or perfecting of the character, as you may wish to call it. This strengthening or perfecting was through obedience.

Note the following:

"Perfection of character is attained through exercise of the faculties of the mind, in times of supreme test, by obedience to every requirement of God's law." —*Testimonies, Series B, No. 9, p. 14.*

"A mere profession of discipleship is of no value. The faith in Christ which saves the soul is not what it is represented to be by many, 'Believe, believe,' they say, 'and you need not keep the law.' But a belief that does not lead to obedience is presumption. The apostle John says, 'He that saith, I know Him, and keepeth not His commandments is a liar, and the truth is not in him.' Let none cherish the idea that special providences of miraculous manifestations are to be the proof of the genuineness of their work or of the ideas they advocate. When persons will speak lightly of the Word of God, and set their impressions, feelings, and exercises above the divine standard, we may know that they have no light in them.

"Obedience is the test of discipleship. It is the keeping of the commandments that proves the sincerity of our professions of love. When the doctrine we accept kills sin in the heart, purifies the soul from defilement, bears fruit unto holiness, we may know that it is the truth of God. When benevolence, kindness, tenderheartedness, sympathy are manifest in our lives; when the joy of rightdoing is in our hearts; when we exalt Christ, and not self, we may know that our faith is of the right order. 'Hereby we do know that we know Him, if we keep His commandments.'" —*Mount of Blessing, pp. 209, 210.*

"There is no genuine sanctification except through obedience to the truth." —*Sanctification, pp. 57.*

*—Righteousness by Faith —What Is It?*

Let it be carefully noted that all the following points in Christian experience are matters of faith—come into the experience by faith. To make a simple analysis of Christian experience, let us outline it as follows:

1. We receive a knowledge of God as Creator, and so of our duty to Him, and then of His law defining our duty, and so a knowledge of our sin—all by faith.

2. We receive a knowledge of the plan of redemption with the offer of pardon on certain conditions; and when those conditions are met, pardon is received—by faith.

3. After receiving the knowledge of duty we must make a decision, to do or not to do. Here is where the will enters into the matter. This is the place for perfect surrender of will, appetite and passions—the

entire being—and we will decide according to what we believe, which is faith in God and His words.

4. Our decision is the motive power of the act, and the act cannot be separated from or be different from the decision that was prompted by the faith without a denial of the faith and reversal of the decision.

5. When we act we put forth every possible effort on our part, and then God adds His almighty power and unites it with our endeavor, and the thing is accomplished. This power from Him comes as a result of two kinds of faith in Him:

    a.    that He will give power as He has said,

    b.    coupled with a faith in His word defining our duty.

Faith is thereby manifested—in putting forth the effort He directs us to put forth to do that which He tells us we ought to do. This effort requires all our energies and time and ability and thought.

If we fail to put forth the effort we thereby deny our faith in one or both of two ways:

    a.    Deny belief in God's outline of our duty;

    b.    Deny belief in His word, which says we must act.

This latter presumes He will add His power even though we do not act, and so turns faith into presumption, and produces a passive experience instead of a warfare; such a faith is "dead being alone." —*James 2:14-26.*

Notice: The power from Him does not come until this point is reached in our experience. It will not come before we act even though we pray for it.

Sample: God did not manifest His power to open the Red Sea until after Israel had lifted up their feet and put them forward, and till they had done so as many times as they could. This of course was a miracle, but it illustrates the time in our experience when God strengthens us.

Therefore, if we believe God's word, such belief will cause us to be righteous and to do righteousness.

*—Perfecting Character*

The particular experience, then, which perfects the character, is the conquest and victory, which is obedience. And the more the faith is tried to accept the duty, to make the decision, and then to act, the more the character is strengthened.

The best character is made when the difficulties surrounding obedience have been well-nigh insurmountable.

## The Holy Spirit and the Latter Rain

The time when God adds His power in our experience, to give us victory, has been misplaced (as stated on pages 23–25 under *Righteousness by Faith*), and confusion has resulted from it, but, because the Spirit is promised both for victory and for power, power for personal victory and power for witnessing have been confused. The distinction is not properly made between the "fruits of the Spirit" and the "gifts of the Spirit," so that the people are being taught to seek for the power of the latter rain to give them victory in the life. For this reason they are confused on their purpose, how they are given, and the time, or order in which given.

The "fruits" and the "gifts" are two distinct manifestations or works of the Spirit. The "fruits"—love, joy, peace etc.—are brought forth in the life of the indi vidual as a result of th e work of the Spirit in his own heart in his Christian experience in connection with surrender, faith, and works and prayer, as set forth in the foregoing pages, for his transformation and salvation. This is the operation of the Spirit to give him victory in his life. Here is where duty, faith, obedience, and prayer come into play.

They first were "holy men" who "spake as they were moved by the Holy Ghost." —2 Peter 1 21 Acts 5.32. Were God to precede victory with power it would be an approval of sin.

But the purpose and work of the "gifts" of the Spirit are altogether different. They are not for the transforming or saving of the individual in whom they are manifested, but are a work of the Spirit through him or the instruction and salvation of others power for witnessing.

They do constitute to him an evidence in his own experience of the correctness of his exper ien ce and in this way they prepare and help him to stand.

When Peter stood up on the day of Pentecost filled with the Spirit, it was not for his salvation but for the salvation of his hearers

The former rain was not given to Peter for his transformation, or for his conversion. All of that was a previous experience with him and was a preparation for the reception of the outpouring of the Spirit with which to work for others. On this point in Peter's experience see *Desire of Ages*, page 812, and *Christ's Object Lessons*, page 154. Also note the following extract:

"The disciples did not ask for a blessing for themselves. They were weighted with the burden of souls. The gospel was to be carried to the ends of the earth, and they claimed the endowment of power that Christ had promised. Then it was that the Holy Spirit was poured out, and thousands were converted in a day.

"So it may be now." —*Testimonies Vol. 8 , 21*

The teaching that the power of the latter rain is to help us to individual personal victory in the life leads people to overlook the real time and also the real experience—the only time and the only experience which can give them victoryand causes them to look forward for victory to a time and to an experience which is not intended to give them victoryand which will not give them victory—and when the time comes to which they are looking, most likely the time and opportunity which God gave them in which to get victory will be past, and then "Oh how many I saw in the time of trouble without a shelter!" —*Early Writings, p. 71.*

Therefore it can be readily seen that this teaching has the same danger and result as that of "second probation" in "Russellism."

Thus the purpose and the time of giving the latter rain are taught erroneously.

The advent movement can never proceed to triumph until a clear message is given and believed and experienced on this subject.

The entire subject of the Holy Spirit and of the latter rain, in their relation to Christian experience, needs to be restudied in both the Bible and Testimonies, and all statements concerning them need to be applied to the one for which they were intended, and each needs to be studied in the light of the other.

We append below a few sample statements to the point that:

*—Victory in the Life Precedes the Latter Rain*

"I saw that none could share the 'refreshing' unless they obtained the victory over every besetment, over pride, selfishness, love of the world, and over every wrong word and action." —*Ibid., p. 71.*

"Not one of us will ever receive the sea] of God while our characters have one spot or stain upon them. It is left with us to remedy the defects in our characters, to cleanse the soul temple of every defilement. Then the latter rain will fall upon us as the early rain fell upon the disciples on the day of Pentecost." —*Testimonies, Vol. 5, p. 214.*

"Those who come up to every point, and stand every test, and overcome, be the price what it may, have heeded the counsel of the True Witness, and they will receive the latter rain, and thus be fitted for translation." —*Ibid., Vol. 1, p. 187.*

"When we bring our hearts into unity with Christ, and our lives into harmony with His work, the Spirit that fell on the disciples on the day of Pentecost will fall on us." —*Ibid., Vol. 8, p. 246.*

"The refreshing or power of God comes only on those who have prepared themselves for it by doing the work which God bids them, namely, cleansing themselves from all filthiness of the flesh and spirit, perfecting holiness in the fear of God." —*Ibid., Vol. 1, p. 619.*

"The latter rain, ripening earth's harvest, represents the spiritual grace that prepares the church for the coming of the Son of Man. But unless the former rain has fallen, there will be no life; the green blade will not spring up. Unless the early showers have done their work, the latter rain can bring no seed to perfection.

"There is to be 'first the blade, then the ear, after that the full corn in the ear.' There must be a constant development of Christian virtue, a constant advancement in Christian experience. This we should seek with intensity of desire, that we may adorn the doctrine of Christ our Saviour.

"Many have in a great measure failed to receive the former rain. They have not obtained all the benefits that God has thus provided for them. They expect that the lack will be supplied by the latter rain. When the richest abundance of grace shall be bestowed, they intend to open their hearts to receive it. They are making a terrible mistake. The work that God has begun in the human heart in giving His light and knowledge must be continually going forward. Every individual must realize his own necessity. The heart must be emptied of every defilement and cleansed for the indwelling of the Spirit. It was by the confession and forsaking of sin, by earnest prayer and consecration of themselves to God, that the early disciples prepared for the outpouring of the Holy Spirit on the day of Pentecost. The same work, only in greater degree, must be done now. Then the human agent had only to ask for the blessing and wait for the Lord to perfect the work concerning him. It is God Who began the work, and He will finish His work, making man complete in Jesus Christ. But there must be no neglect of the grace represented by the former rain. Only those who are living up to the light they have will receive greater light. Unless we are daily advancing in the exemplification of the active Christian virtues, we shall not recognize the manifestations of the Holy Spirit in the latter rain. It may be failing on hearts all

around us, but we shall not discern or receive it."
—*Review and Herald, March 2, 1897, and Atlantic Union Gleaner, June 22, 1910.*

# Health Reform

Health reform is given a large place in God's plan of our experiencing the victorious life. We cannot get righteousness by a faith that denies health reform.

That this may be made perfectly clear we append the following quotations to the point:

"The health reform, I was shown, is a part of the third angel's message....I saw that we as people must make an advance move in this great work....God's people are not prepared for the loud cry of the third angel. They have a work to do for themselves which they should not leave for God to do for them....Lustful appetite makes slaves of men and women, and beclouds their intellects and stupefies their moral sensibilities to such a degree that the sacred elevated truths of God's word are not appreciated." —*Testimonies, Vol. 1, p. 486.*

"The controlling power of appetite will prove the ruin of thousands, when, if they had conquered on this point, they would have had moral power to gain the victory over every other temptation of Satan. But those who are slaves to appetite will fail in perfecting Christian character....As we near the close of time Satan's temptation to indulge appetite will be more powerful and more difficult to overcome." —*Ibid., Vol. 3, pp. 491, 492.*

"It is impossible for those who indulge the appetite to attain to Christian perfection." —*Ibid., Vol. 2, p. 400.*

"God demands that the appetites be cleansed, and that self-denial be practiced in regard to those things which are not good. This is a work that will have to be done before His people can stand before Him a perfected people." —*Ibid., Vol. 9, pp. 153, 154.*

The rejection of the place obedience to health reform has in the Christian experience, coupled with the desire for the power of the "gifts" to get victory, naturally produces a desire to secure health by miraculous means instead of by obedience.

Because of the situation we have already described, this deception most naturally besets the ministry.

And so there is among us as a people a desire for miraculous healing not after God's order, and which is already proving a snare to some of us.

Many are looking to miracles (healing among the rest) as a result or evidence of the latter rain, and so as a confirmation that our message and movement are inspired of God. All such are on dangerous ground, and have already opened the door to the enemy to present to them one of the most insidious and disastrous deceptions in store for this people.

In this age when the work of God is to be finished and a people made ready to meet Him, God has not ordained that the rank and file of His people shall receive miraculous physical healing in time of sickness. While He does not today desire to exclude miraculous healing, yet in this matter He has put a difference between these and apostolic days.

"The way in which Christ worked was to preach the word, and to relieve suffering by miraculous works of healing. But I am instructed that we cannot now work in this way; for Satan will exercise his power by working miracles. God's servants today could not work by means of miracles, because spurious works of healing, claiming to be divine, will be wrought.

"For this reason the Lord has marked out a way in which His people are to carry forward a work of physical healing, combined with the teaching of the word. Sanitariums are to be established, and with these institutions are to be connected workers who will carry foward genuine medical missionary work." —*Unpublished Testimonies, MS., pp. 53-54.*

"Christ is no longer in this world in person, to go through our cities and towns and villages, healing the sick; but He has commissioned us to carry forward the medical missionary work that He began. In this work we are to do our very best. Institutions for the care of the sick are to be established, where men and women suffering from disease may be placed under the care of God-fearing physicians and nurses, and be treated without drugs." —*Testimonies, Vol. 9, p. 168.*

One reason why God does not now make miraculous healing the main dependence is that it does not give the necessary aid in perfecting character, and character is the only thing that prepares us for the latter rain or translation.

Obedience is the thing that develops character, and to make perfect character the obedience must include both the spiritual and physical life and habits. And if God should heal us miraculously of sickness caused by our own transgression and in the midst of our transgression, He would thereby set His seal to our sins, and as a result we would be confirmed in our sins rather than led away from them, and the preparation for the latter rain and for translation hindered rather than furthered.

If we could cure through the "gift of healing" every sick person who comes to us and who is in our midst, that would not assist God in His great task of getting characters ready for translation. Rather it would hinder Him in doing so. It would cause the people to look lightly upon obedience to physical law, and upon their physical sins, and would prevent their putting them away, and thus prevent the development of character.

If we were only living in obedience as evangelical workers and as medical workers and people, then God could add the miraculous healing without compromising Himself; but because of our continual trangression—living in sin—He cannot bestow the miraculous without thereby approving of our sins. Our obedience must come first. On this point note the following quotation:

"After Christ's baptism He preached the gospel to the cities that were round about. He was working and healing —the medical missionary work was bound up with the preaching of the gospel.... You may say, 'Why not, then, take hold of the work and heal the sick as Christ did?' I answer, "You are not ready." Some have believed, some have been healed, but there are many who make themselves sick by intemperate eating or indulging in other wrong habits. When they get sick, shall we pray for them to be raised up, that they may carry on the very same work again? There must be a reformation throughout our ranks; the people must reach a higher standard before we expect the power of God to be manifested in a marked manner for the healing of the sick.... Let me tell you that the sick will be healed when you have faith to come to God in the right way." —*General Conference Bulletin, 1901, pp. 25, 26.*

Consequently the basis of God's true healing in this movement, whether miraculous or otherwise, must be, first of all, obedience to both spiritual and physical laws.

Therefore, we must not look to this generation for a wholesale and promiscuous healing of the people such as was done by Christ and the apostles. The church then was not facing the issue of preparing for translation. Because the church now must prepare characters for translation, a different process is employed to do much of the healing work. By the Spirit of Prophecy the work of healing by teaching and treatment is classed as the same work that Christ did miraculously.

Thus the physicians and nurses in this movement are planned by God to be educators, teaching obedience not merely for the sake of health in this life, but for the sake of character and health eternally; and this is their highest calling.

This work of teaching is as sacred as was the miraculous healing Christ did 1900 years ago, and is to achieve even more exalted ends. This thought, when received, will shut out of our healing work the employment of any method not in harmony with this sacred purpose. This kind of healing can be done only by workers as fully sanctified as those who did the miraculous healing of 1900 years ago.

Without this conception of the healing principles, the teaching of what we usually term "spiritual truths" will be done in a way that will surely lead to a misconception of faith; will unbalance the relation between faith and works, and so lead to an unsound Christian experience; to seeking the latter rain on a false premise, and so to the loss of our souls.

God knew what He was doing when He made the health message a part of the third angel's message. Neither the ministry nor the medical workers can have a balanced experience or present a balanced message without the part of the message the other represents. Each is necessary to the other.

Our movement cannot proceed to the triumph until we unite on this ground. Satan knows this, and he is playing for all our souls over this question. Those who sooner or later do not obtain the correct understanding of God's purpose in the closing work to heal by natural methods, of which obedience is the basis, and come into harmony with this will sooner or later surely be taken in the snare of some sort of miraculous healing; for those who are seeking for the power of healing which is against the plan of God are liable to have their desires for such power gratified from an undesirable source.

## Satanic Deceptions Among SDAs

It is possible for Seventh-day Adventists to follow error till they have gone so far from the right track (remember how close together lie the track of truth and the track of error) that they will seek the power of the "gifts" in a way contrary to God's specifications. If they persist in this they thereby become candidates to receive power from the same source as the error came which they are following, though they may know it not. They are then looking to the wrong source, and the following statement applies to them as fully as to other Protestants who are looking to the wrong leader.

"Like the Jews, who offered their useless sacrifices, they offer up their useless prayers to the apartment which Jesus has left; and Satan, pleased with the deception, assumes a religious character, and leads the minds of these professed Christians to himself, working with his power, his signs and lying wonders, to fasten them in his snare. Some he deceives in one way, and some in another. He has different delusions prepared to affect different minds. Some look with horror upon one deception, while they readily receive another. Satan deceives some with Spiritualism. He also comes as an angel of light and spreads his influence over the land by means of false reformations. The churches are elated, and consider that God is working marvelously for them, when it is the work of another spirit." —*Early Writings, p. 261.*

And the same is true of the statement next quoted from *Early Writings.* Satan knows better than to stake very much on deceiving Seventh-day Adventists with open Spiritualism, and a far better plan is to introduce among us a false latter rain by getting the people to seek God for the latter rain on a basis which He does not authorize, and so receive something which they think is the Holy Ghost but which is not that. While the following statement refers to those "who have rejected the truth," the same principles must apply to those among us who have rejected truth—who are in error and are under the delusions of Satan.

"I saw that Satan was working through agents in a number of ways. He was at work through ministers who have rejected the truth and are given over to strong delusions to believe a lie that they might be damned. While they were preaching or praying some would fall prostrate and helpless, not by the power of the Holy Ghost, but by the power of Satan breathed upon these agents, and through them to the people. While preaching, praying or conversing, some professed Adventists who had rejected present truth used mesmerism to gain adherents, and the people would rejoice in this influence, for they thought it was the Holy Ghost. Some even that used it were so far in the darkness and deception of the devil that they thought it was the power of God, given them to exercise. They had made God altogether such an one as themselves and had valued His power as a thing of naught." —*Early Writings, pp. 43,44.*

The next quotation is concerning Seventh-day Adventists who have followed the promptings of their own hearts rather than the voice of God:

"...the voice of Satan is so disguised that it is accepted as the voice of God." —*Testimonies, Vol. 5, p. 512.*

In this connection the following statement is full of significance:

"Do not forget that the most dangerous snares which Satan has prepared for the church will come through its own members who do not love God supremely or their neighbors as themselves." *Ibid., p. 477.*

A statement is now introduced which shows that the rejecting of the light of the health message places the rejector where he is exposed to the delusions of Satan.

"God has placed it in our power to obtain a knowledge of the laws of health. He has made it our duty to preserve our physical powers in the best possible condition, that we may render to Him acceptable service. Those who refuse to improve the light and knowledge that have been mercifully placed within their reach are rejecting one of the means which God has granted them to promote spiritual as well as physical life. They are placing themselves where they will be exposed to the delusions of Satan." —*Testimonies, Vol. 5, p. 193.*

# Power Before Character

## Substitute Preparation for the Latter Rain

The position being taken concerning receiving the latter rain before victory involves a different procedure than to obtain the latter rain from what God has given us, as well as teaching a false victorious life. Because it places power before character, it must present something else as a preparation in place of victory, which is God's appointed preparation.

Now the devil knows that all Seventh-day Adventists understand the gospel pretty well, and so the best deception he can invent as a substitute preparation for the latter rain is a partial truth which will give a deficient experience. There he tells us we can get it by prayer.

Now prayer is right, and to pray for the Holy Spirit in the life to give us victory is right, and to pray for the latter rain is right when all the conditions have been met. All this is clearly taught in the Bible and in the *Testimonies*. This is truth, but is a partial truth. Prayer is but one spoke in the wheel of the whole experience necessary to become ready for the latter rain; and he deceives men into thinking that this one spoke is the whole wheel.

This thing is cropping out more and more in our midst. As a sample of it we have the *Rowan Movement* which is just this thing, pure and simple. This is the predominating thing in it—getting the power by prayer, placing the getting of the power as the objective when the getting of character should be the objective. This is Satan's purpose in that movement. His object is to lead Seventh-day Adventists into error.

His primary purpose is not to exalt a woman; he is exalting the woman as a means only of exalting the error.

There are places where Rowanism is not being successfully met and overthrown. To bring evidence that she is a false prophet is one thing; but this error, which is the foundation of that movement, is so common among our people that it gives her definitive ground upon which to stand; and after people have learned from her this false idea of the latter rain they will still hold it in their hearts regardless of how they view her, because they think it is orthodox, Thus the iniquity of the thing steadily gains ground. The devil might even be willing men should reject her if they would still hold to this fatal error. There must be a deeper insight into this and a more thorough work done. Their emissaries are in many of our churches and are very diligent at all this sort of an experience in getting the latter rain. They are having a deep experience of some kind; they know they have gotten something. There is a power of some kind in their work. It is either the power of God or of the devil. If of the devil, it gives them an experience which is a terribly dangerous substitute for a right experience. You may deny that they have healing or prophecy, but it cannot be denied that they get an "experience"; and they cannot be convinced that this "experience" is not of God because they got it by prayer. It is more important that we correctly analyze the experience she had than it is to get our eyes fixed on the predictions that she made, and that may possibly even come true. If a prophet leads away from God, follow him not, even though his predictions happen to come true.

This thing is so clever that some of the literature they put out is exceedingly pious and deeply spiritual and contains no error except that it is deficient in vital things in that it does not point out the besetting sins and so is lacking the elements of reform that will change the heart. This is the only thing by which some of their literature can be detected as error.

The writer met a thing of this same sort some eight years ago. A band of our ministers made a terribly arnest attempt to get the power of the latter rain by prayer and confession and unity (half of the wheel). Their theology had no place in it for health reform and consequently the relation between faith and works was upset and their experience unsound. But they sought God till they got an "experience" different from anything they had ever had before; they knew it was different, and others knew it was different; and they went about the country leading others into the same "experience" and scattering confusion and ultimate discouragement where they went. The president of the General Conference was a party to this attempt to get the "power." Elder A, the leader of this party, has been more or less crooked in teaching and theology and experience since, and until this day. In an interview just a few days before the recent General Conference session the writer raised the question of the need of victory before the latter rain, and this leader admitted that such was the need and that that thought ought to be made the biggest thing at the coming conference, but that it could not be done because the people and leaders did not want it, as they wanted men to talk about getting the power, and so he helped to carry through the General Conference program as described later in these pages. What an admission of having sold his conscience to meet the demand of the leaders of this people, and to maintain his popularity. A Rowanite sister recently told the writer that their literature contains the same teaching concerning the latter rain as was taught by the above-mentioned Elder A, now a General Conference laborer going to all parts of the United States. We did not suppose she knew it, but we did, before she mentioned it. So Mrs. Rowan and they are working hand in hand even though they think she is teaching error.

## A False or Substitute Sealing Work

We have therefore false views substituted for the true in all of the following, and so have:

a.    A false diagnosis of our condition
b.    A false reformation
c.    A false Christian experience
d.    A false faith
e.    A false victorious life
f.    A false righteousness by faith
g.    A false preparation for latter rain
h.    A false latter rain
i.    A false sealing

All of these have been elucidated in the foregoing pages with the exception of the last named, and it is now proposed to deal with it.

There is one important feature of the sealing work which is not usually explained. After an individual has been sealed by God he does not change. This is not entirely an edict of God which forbids his changing, but this individual has had something in his own experience which confirmed him, fixed, and established him and settled him forever in the thing he has espoused. Those who espouse the full blaze of the gospel light shining upon the remnant church will be confirmed, or sealed in it. How is it done?

The truth is to impart an experience to each receiver, but it is not enough that the receiver have a right experience; he must know that the experience is right. This is a most vital point. He must become convinced beyond all controversy that it is right! He must become so sure of it that he will stand to it though the heavens fall!

We have a most wonderful example of this principle in the experience of Christ. One of the most trying temptations that came to Him in His earthly life was the one of believing in His own experience: Was He the Son of God or was He not? The devil always dogged His steps with that doubt. Practically all the evidence would indicate that He was not. The mystery of His mission had to unfold to Him when He began to come to the years of accountability. He had to read the scriptures for Himself and find Himself there and take His nature, His mission, His work, and therefore His experience as a matter of faith. The crisis of the test of His faith on this point was on the cross when He had been rejected by the heathen, by His own people; when His followers had "gone back"; His disciples had fled; His relatives had discredited Him—, Judas had sold Him; ardent Peter had denied Him; angels had left Him; the Holy Spirit was withdrawn; and then His Father withdrew. Then Satan pointed that question at Him for the last time: Do you still think you are the Son of Heaven? Through all these experiences He had something to hold Him; He had been confirmed and established in His experience by something from without His experience. At His baptism God had spoken to Him and said, "This is my beloved Son in whom I am well pleased." And on the mount of transfiguration the same voice had repeated the same words. The miracles which God had wrought through His ministry were a mighty confirmation of His experience. And so it is written in *Desire of Ages*, page 756:

"Amid the awful darkness, apparently forsaken of God, Christ had drained the last dregs in the cup of human woe. In those dreadful hours He had relied upon the evidence of His Father's acceptance heretofore given Him."

Thus it is when God bestows a special manifestation of the "gifts" in an individual for the salvation of his hearers, this special manifestation to the individual is a witness of the approval of God upon his experience, and settles and establishes him in it—confirms and seals him in it. Notice the distinction herein made between developing his character and confirming him in his experience through which the character was developed. Without this distinction there is an apparent contradiction in *Early Writings*, page 71, where we find these two seemingly opposing statements:

"I saw that many were neglecting the preparation so needful and were looking to the time of 'refreshing' and the 'latter rain' to fit them to stand in the day of the Lord and to live in His sight. Oh, how many I saw in the time of trouble without a shelter!"

Then in the next sentence it speaks of the refreshing "that all must have to live in the sight of a holy God."

The thought taught in this last quoted statement is the one with which we are dealing just now. The latter rain brings special manifestations of the power of God in the "gifts" which constitute a witness, assurance, and evidence which confirms and seals us in our experience and so makes us steadfast during the time of Jacob's trouble and during the time when there is no intercessor.

But—let it be noted at this point—it is just as possible and easy to be sealed in an error as in the truth! The same identical principle applies. Eddyites are confirmed or sealed in their belief and doctrine by the miraculous power in their work. The same is true of spiritualists, and many others. This is why it is so hard to convert one of them.

All the souls in the world are to be confirmed either in truth or error by miraculous evidences. They will be confirmed in their experience so that you cannot change their minds and their course—thus they will be sealed.

Those who are sealed by God will be sealed by His Spirit (*Ephesians 1:13, 4:30*). The bestowal of the "gifts" under the latter rain will seal them in the experience they have had in the development of the "fruits." They cannot be sealed, however, until they have become obedient. The Sabbath is the seal because it is the sign of perfect obedience to the Creator because He is the Creator. The seal that signifies perfect obedience will never be placed upon those of whom God continues to say, "Their taste, their appetite, is their god"; and finally "God will soon say to His angels: Let them alone." (*Testimonies*, Vol. 1, p. 486.) And so the Sabbath truth carries with it the gospel of health.

Therefore a false latter rain (manifestations of Satanic power among professed Seventh-day Adventists) will result in a false sealing. This is exactly what the Rowanism offers, as may be seen from her document entitled, *The Steps in the Process of the Infilling*. But this false sealing does not end with Rowanism; it will go wherever error is retained in place of truth and obedience to it; and according to this thesis it will sweep into its grasp a host of Seventh-day Adventists.

All of the foregoing lends great emphasis to the fact that to be deceived in one's own experience is the very worst of all possible calamities and the most difficult from which to find deliverance.

"'What stronger delusion can beguile the mind than the pretense that you are building on the right foundation and that God accepts your works, when in reality you are working out many things according to worldly policy and are sinning against Jehovah? Oh, it is a great deception, a fascinating delusion, that takes possession of minds when men who have once known the truth mistake the form of godliness for the spirit and power thereof; when they suppose that they are rich and increased with goods and in need of nothing, while in reality they are in need of everything.'" —*Ibid., Vol. 8, p. 249.*

"The knowledge of our state, as God views it, seems to be hidden from us. We see, but perceive not; we hear, but do not understand; and we rest as unconcerned as if the pillar of cloud by day, and the pillar of fire by night, rested upon our sanctuary. We profess to know God, and to believe the truth; but in works deny Him. Our deeds are directly adverse to the principles of truth and righteousness, by which we profess to be governed." —*Testimonies, Vol. 5, p. 84.*

### *How Far Has It Gone?*

It has gone so far that workers can hardly give a discourse on Christian experience in harmony with the thoughts of this thesis in the presence of other workers and not at once become "marked" and branded as a "fanatic" or as "departed from the faith." So many have departed from the faith—many unwittingly—that so far as the majority are concerned the departure from the faith has come to be considered orthodox, and the man who still stands by "the faith once delivered to the saints" is liable to be branded as a fanatic and declared to be unsound and unsafe.

The fact is an alarming number of our educators, preachers, evangelists, and writers are into this thing. Many of the sermons and articles of today on these subjects are tainted with it. Revival efforts are commonly conducted after this sort. The workers in the United States being so saturated with it, the inevitable consequence is that the men sent abroad carry it there. Consequently our work among all people has been strongly influenced in this direction from the United States and has the same effect in other lands (upon native people and all) upon the Christian experience and general spiritual condition.

While God is saying, "If we would elevate the moral standard of any country where we may be called to go, we must begin by correcting the physical habits of the people" (*Healthful Living, par. 1140*), the administration even takes the stand that in some countries health reform is not a practical subject especially in the matter of diet. How many souls will be lost to the kingdom as a result, and who will answer for it at the bar of God?

Another form in which this thing manifests itself is in the lack of interest in and even opposition to the establishment of treatment rooms and restaurants in the large cities, a thing for which God called for many years.

Still again we can see the same thing in the decrease in the number of sanitariums while God is calling for more of them in this country and for their establishment in all countries.

Again, the same thing shows itself in lack of interest in or opposition to medical evangelism, the union of the spiritual and health work in evangelistic efforts.

Much of the writing of many of our leading men today is so near like the writing of general Protestant writers who do not believe this message and even oppose it that their writings are quoted as freely as or more so than is the Spirit of Prophecy, indicating to some extent from what source they draw their inspiration. This has gone on until there is a strong tendency to "hush up" the message and take the keen edge off it. Men fear this man and that organization; they are careful about saying those things that put all men under condemnation and show that men reject the vital cutting truths of this message at the loss of their souls.

Our preachers usually are not theologians, but administrators, which is contrary to God's specific and oft-repeated instruction (read *Testimonies, Vol. 7, pp. 246–252*). They are so occupied with running the conferences as a business and planning and putting through conference programs that they do not have time to know the message or secure a deep heart experience in it. And so it happens that our preachers as administrators and officials are using the machinery and organization of the denomination to promote this apostasy.

The objective of this program is to get the "power" of the latter rain while ignoring health reform in Christian experience and character building, and while ignoring the fact that character and victory must come before the latter rain rather than after.

## *The General Conference*

This has been the trend since we parted company with Doctor Kellogg, and the trend has now become so strong that the program of the recent General Conference session was planned in advance and was organized and operated, and the machinery of the organization used, in an attempt to get the "power" at that meeting.

That such was the case may be clearly seen from the announcements published in the *Review and Herald*, and from the announcement distributed through the Union papers, from circulars and from the reports of the Conference published in the *Review and Herald* and in the *Bulletin*.

A General Conference officer personally told the writer at Loma Linda a few days before the Conference that never in our history had such extensive and perfect plans been laid to so conduct a meeting that an outpouring of the latter rain might be received.

The following was published in the *Review and Herald* of April 27, 1922:

"We must obtain what is needed to help us reach and save the poor lost people in every land to which the providence of God shall lead us from this meeting. We must go forth filled with the Holy Spirit, which we are assured by the Spirit of Prophecy will 'bring all other blessings in its train.'"

This, it will be seen, is subject to either a right or wrong interpretation. If the right "preparation" had been offered, no fault could now be found with this announcement; but the "preparation" that was offered was prayer, confession, and unity, and all of these were used erroneously so their function was perverted, as we have already set forth in these pages. The "prayer" ignored divine essentials in the program of receiving the outpouring. The "confession" seemed to be aimed very largely at soliciting confessions of "criticisms." While this was no doubt much needed, yet it was made to cover also a confession or rather retraction of earnest protests which the administration persisted in regarding as evil criticism. The unity, while professing to be a unity with God, was really a demand upon men to line up with the administration. Thus these three would-be preparations for and conditions to receiving the outpouring were all counterfeits.

## A Call to Intercession

In a circular entitled *An Important Meeting* sent out by the General Conference in March 1922, announcing the coming general conference session, appears the following:

"Let us advance upon our knees.

"From the lips of every true-hearted believer in this message there should daily go forth most earnest prayer from the family altar and from the secret place, that this gathering shall be characterized by a mighty outpouring of the Holy Spirit and that all who are there may be led into a victorious experience over sin, and may return to their fields to carry the message in the power of the Spirit.

"Should we not see a spirit of intercession such as was manifested before the day of Pentecost?

"God is willing to give us a great spiritual refreshing at the time of our coming General Conference. Let us confess our sins, and so humble our hearts that this work which is to enlighten the world may begin in our midst."

Two points stand out in this very clearly:

a.   The plan and hope were to get a "mighty outpouring" at "this gathering."

b.   The result was to be a "victorious experience over sin."

The following appeared in the *Review* of May 18, 1922: "Men may stand in the way of great blessings during this Conference. Realizing this, many are offering daily intercession in behalf of the meeting. They are praying that God will help all who attend to humble their hearts and renounce everything that might prevent our receiving a real Pentecostal blessing.

"From all directions I am receiving letters full of solicitude for the Conference. Some of them bring tears to my eyes. All express a deep conviction that the supreme need of our people and our cause is a great spiritual revival, that our greatest need in this Conference is to be filled with the Holy Spirit as the disciples were on the day of Pentecost. For this our people are praying."

Truly, men stood in the way, but those who most stood in the way apparently knew it not.

In the *Review and Herald* of May 22, 1922, pages 4 and 5, and in the *Bulletin*, pages 14 and 15, appear these statements:

"But after all this, He commanded them to remain where they were, in the city of Jerusalem, until they received power from on high. Said He, 'Ye shall receive power, when the Holy Ghost is come upon you.'

"The disciples followed their Lord's instruction to the letter, and He kept His promise. He sent the Holy Spirit to them. He endued them with power. Then they began to speak, and what a marvelous power attended them! Soon they were in the whirl of a great movement, but at every step and turn that same mighty power wrought for them. They were triumphant everywhere. Opposition, difficulties, hindrances of every description, went down before these witnesses for Christ.

"My brethren, the church of Christ and a world facing utter chaos need a repetition of apostolic experiences. We have the same gospel to preach. We have the same world to warn. We have the same divine commission. We need the same mighty power in our church today. Ministers and Bible workers need the power of the Holy Spirit to send conviction to the hearts of those whom they instruct. Fathers and mothers need power from God to live victorious lives in their homes. Our dear young greatly need power from above to enable them to resist the overmastering allurements and temptations of this corrupt time. And how seriously our missionaries need divine help and power to cope with the forces of evil in the lands of superstition and darkness to which they are called. How greatly, too, do they need help from above to protect them from the deadly diseases to which they are exposed. Alas, how utterly we shall fail without this heavenly enduement! But with it we shall be victorious. We are assured by the Spirit of Prophecy that 'when divine power is combined with human effort, the work will spread like fire in the stubble. God will employ agencies whose origin men will be unable to discern.' This is just what thousands of our people want to see manifested. Many are seriously troubled and depressed because they do not see and experience the working of this divine influence as they feel they have reason to expect, and they are looking to this Conference for something to take place that will bring new life and power to the people of God."

The president in his address, as appeared in the *Review*, read a letter received from one of our ministers in which letter were the following statements:

"Should not this General Conference be the Pentecost of the third angel's message?...I shall unite my heart with many thousands of others in seeking God that He may pour upon you a Pentecostal blessing....

"These statements express what is pressing hardest upon the hearts of our loyal people everywhere. They are not greatly concerned about the program and the resolutions and the many other details of the Conference. They want God to come near and give us a signal blessing. They want a mighty movement to start here that will sweep through the world, helping our own people to live victorious lives, and causing the honest in heart everywhere to come quickly into the fold of the remnant church."

That this man was understood to teach as we have stated is manifested from the note about his address, which note appeared in the *Review and Herald* of May 22, 1922, page 16, as follows:

"Elder...read the President's quadrennial address, a copy of which will be found on the third page of this number of the *Review*. The speaker emphasized the great need of more spiritual power in our hearts, and counseled that all our believers pray without ceasing for the outpouring which 'brings all other blessings in its train.'"

As there was a strong possibility that the administration, which has been in authority since the days of separation from Doctor Kellogg, and which administration received the "bent" toward the *omega* under the *alpha* at that time would terminate at the recent Conference, and as other attempts had been made by said administration to get the "power" by the wrong process, it was to be expected that the getting of the "power" at this time by such a process would be sought, and everything would be bent in that direction to accomplish that thing as a crowning achievement; and the receiving of it would constitute a vindication that the administration of twenty-one years was right in these things and had been working along right lines, and that the Spirit of Prophecy could be ignored in certain vital matters while professing to accept it as a gift in the church; that victory is not necessary before the latter rain; that health reform is not necessary to victory; that righteousness by faith may ignore the place given of God to "works."

It is a notable fact that the General Conference session was not marked by any special power or blessing in a spiritual way more than any similar gathering, but rather by less. And so from the standpoint of these plans laid for (the purpose in it, and the hope for it), it was practically a failure. A leading officer said at the Conference: "This is the most wonderful meeting we as a people have ever held." Wonderful it truly was in attendance, in opportunity, and in lack of spiritual power. Since the conference some have continued to lay the lack of spiritual power in the meeting to the so-called "politics" played by those who opposed his reelection, and have become the champions of a great revival and reformatory movement to be conducted along the erroneous lines laid out in these pages. Beware of the spiritual revival and reformations brought to the people by such methods and teaching.

Thank God that no manifestation of "power" was seen at the General Conference, for when the "power" is given on this program it will be the most subtle and deceptive thing this denomination has ever seen. Those who receive it will claim that those who do not join with them in it are rejecting the Spirit of God; and will quote such testimonies to them (which has already been done) as the following:

"It may be falling on hearts all around us, but we shall not discern or receive it." —*Review and Herald*, March 2, 1897 and *Atlantic Union Gleaner*, June 22, 1922.

"There is to be in the churches a wonderful manifestation of the power of God, but it will not move upon those who have not humbled themselves before the Lord and opened the door of their heart by confession and repentance. In the manifestation of that Power which lightens the earth wi th the glory of God, they will see only something which in their blindness they think dangerous, something which will arouse their fears, and they will brace themselves to resist it. Because the Lord does not work according to their expectations and ideas, they will oppose the work. 'Why,' they say, 'should we not know the Spirit of God, when we have been in the work so many years?' Because they did not respond to the warnings, the entreaties, of the messages of God, but persistently said, 'I am rich, and increased with goods, and have need of nothing.'" —*Mrs. E. G. White, Bible Training School, May 1907.*

Those who receive this power will be deceived, and will say that they obtained the "power" through prayer and therefore it must be divine. Such experiences as these will come much nearer deceiving the "elect" than anything we have ever met before. These things will try men's souls. Those who reject this thing will be counted as against the organization; against the leaders,—against the manifestation of the latter rain; and so against the Spirit of God and against God; and so will be absolutely denounced!

The *alpha* apostasy left the "road" on the right side, so to speak, and the *omega* leaves the straight road on the opposite or left-hand side. Therefore, by the very nature of the case, any man who seeks to draw people back to the middle of the road will be charged by the *omega* people with leading men back to the *alpha* apostasy because the middle of the road is halfway between the *alpha* and the *omega*. The writer knows what it is to be so charged (notes can be supplied from the General Conference speaker's talk which supports this).

## Criticism

Those who reject the apostasy will be severely charged with criticism because they will protest against it. A great effort has been made for a long time to eliminate "criticism." It has been terribly condemned far and near—in sermons, articles, conventions, institutes, campmeetings and conferences. Honest protest has been stifled and suppressed by branding it "criticism" and then condemning it.

A distinction must be made between "protest" and "criticism," for if not, no voice can be raised against wrong! Pernicious criticism is a wicked thing, and ought to be confessed and forsaken. Criticism of men is that bad. But there is another side to this question of criticism.

If men have gone so far in criticism that they criticize the work of the Spirit of God and the messages from the Spirit of God and denounce those who are maintaining those messages as having the spirit of the devil, that would come terribly close to being a sin against the Holy Spirit and would call for alarm and utter humiliation and abasement before such men should dare lift up their heads and ask God for the gift of His Holy Spirit in the latter rain.

This criticism of the work of the Spirit of God is more heinous and disastrous to ourselves and to the work of God than is criticism of men.

If leaders so criticize the Spirit of Prophecy that men are moved by the Spirit of God to protest against such apostasy, there must be a distinction made between such protest and evil criticism. When men are in the wrong and do not see it and God sends brethren to counsel them and they persist in denouncing such counsel as unjust criticism, they are indeed in a great delusion, and it is most difficult for God to reach them

According to Inspiration there will be various voices in the church from this time forward till after the shaking is over. There will be false reformations that will sweep in thousands; there will be great worldliness and there will be those who "sigh and cry" over the condition of the church as God sees it, and these will reprove and warn and "will not hold their peace to obtain the favor of any." These are the ones who will be sealed. Notwithstanding their earnest efforts, they will be "powerless to stop the rushing torrent of iniquity" (*Testimonies, Vol. 5, p. 210*), because the majority join in the general apostasy and refuse to heed the reproofs. They will be misjudged and denounced and "scourged" by men in "responsible positions" (*Ibid., p. 79*), "guardians of the spiritual interests of the people" who have "betrayed their trust" (*Ibid., p. 211*), "destroyers" who have for many years been "training under the hand of Satan and only wait the departure of a few more standard bearers" like Elder _____ to bring the day "when holy hands bear the ark no longer" and when "woe will be upon the people" who are led astray by their unfaithful shepherds (*Ibid., p. 77*). These true "protestants" will pass through a trying time—a "tarrying time" (*Ibid., p. 81*)—and where "there are no faithful ministers," and "where the shepherds are not true, God will take charge of the flock Himself" (*Ibid., p. 80*). These "protestants" will hold to their trying position till there comes a change of leaders—when "Those who have proved themselves unfaithful will not be entrusted with the flock. In the last solemn work few great men will be engaged. They are self-sufficient, independent of God, and He cannot use them" (*Ibid., p. 80*). And then it will come to pass that the true ones "may be the last to offer the gospel of peace to our unthankful churches" (*Ibid., p. 77*); the true ones do the last work for the churches, for "the Lord has faithful servants who in the shaking, testing time will be disclosed to view." They are "precious ones now hidden" (*Ibid. pp 80, 81*). It may be they are said to be "hidden" because the leaders have sought to remove their contact and so their influence from the people. While these faithful ones give the solemn warnings, those who oppose it and rise up against it, the "conservative class" (*Ibid., p. 463*), bear a message which God denotes a "peace and safety" cry in the church. The reader will find the "peace and safety" message and its opposite in such passages as *Testimonies*, Vol, 5, pp. 83, 104, 211, Vol. 2, pp. 252, 254, 257; Vol. 8, p. 250.

The shaking, let it be noticed, is not said to be caused by the voice of the prophet who is dead, but rather by the "straight testimony called forth" from those who received the "counsel of the True Witness to the Laodiceans. This will have its effect upon the heart of the receiver, and will lead him to exalt the standard and pour forth the straight truth. Some will not bear this straight testimony. They will rise up against it, and this is what will cause a shaking among God's people" (*Early Writings, p. 270*). These true "protestants" hold to their stand on "the commandments of God and the Testimony of Jesus Christ" —absolute obedience to God and to His Voice in the Spirit of Prophecy; this is the issue; this is the true standard; the departure from this standard is the apostasy, and there never was and never will be any apostasy other than such, because there can be no other, as that is what apostasy is.

Those who have been drawn into the apostasy through the process of time, and who "rise up against" the "straight testimony" will depart from the folds of the church when the persecution from the world becomes bitter through the enforcement of Sunday laws. "In this time the gold will be separated from the dross in the church" (*Testimonies, Vol. 5, p. 81*). This will purge and cleanse the church from its "dross" and open the way for the latter rain to come in its fullness (read *Early Writings, pp. 269,271*). But now "God's displeasure is upon His people, and He will not manifest His power in the midst of them while sins exist among them and are fostered by those in responsible positions," —*Testimonies, Vol. 3, p. 270.*

## *Unity*

We hear much said about coming into unity; but what is the unity called for? That you should cease differing from and opposing us, and our program and our policies. While calling for unity, the true basis of unity in this movement is being destroyed—belief in the Spirit of Prophecy. To profess to believe it counts for but little while such profession is denied by refusal for years to follow its instruction.

Mere unity among ourselves, though it might be perfect unity, is not the thing needed. We must become united to Christ. This includes knowing His voice as He speaks to the remnant church as the only basis of unity in this inspired movement, knowing His program for this hour, and coming into harmony with it. Such unity includes, among many other things, what He has said about health reform being an "important aid" to obtaining the victory over sin and so being a part of the preparation for the latter rain and for translation into His kingdom. Let our unity be union with God and with His plans for His remnant church.

Unity with leaders merely, might be disastrous, for God has spoken many serious things about "leaders" in this movement, a few of which are quoted herein.

"Satan's chief work is at the headquarters of our faith. He spares no pains to corrupt men in responsible positions and to persuade them to be unfaithful to their several trusts." —*Ibid., Vol. 4, pp. 210, 211.*

"Many a star that we have admired for its brilliancy will then go out in darkness." —*Ibid., Vol. 5, p. 81.*

"The Lord has shown me that men in responsible positions are standing directly in the way of His work, because they think the work must be done and the blessing must come in a certain way, and they will not recognize that which comes in any other way. My brethren, may the Lord place this matter before you as it is. God does not work as men plan, or as they wish; He 'moves in a mysterious way His wonders to perform.' Why reject the Lord's methods of working because they do not coincide with our ideas? God has His appointed channels of light, but these are not necessarily the minds of any particular set of men. When all shall take their appointed place in God's work, earnestly seeking wisdom and guidance from Him, then a great advance will have been made toward letting light shine upon the world. When men shall cease to place themselves in the way, God will work among us as never before." —*Testimonies, Vol. 5, p. 726.*

"Special instruction has been given me for God's people, for perilous times are upon us. In the world, destruction and violence are increasing. In the church, man power is gaining the ascendency; those who have been chosen to occupy positions of trust think it their prerogative to rule.

"Men whom the Lord calls to important positions in His work are to cultivate a humble dependence upon Him. They are not to seek to embrace too much authority; for God has not called them to a work of ruling, but to plan and counsel with their fellow laborers. Every worker alike is to hold himself amenable to the requirements and instructions of God." —*Ibid., Vol. 9, p. 270,*

"Some of our leading brethren have frequently taken their position on the wrong side; and if God would send a message and wait for these older brethren to open the way for its advancement it would never reach the people. These brethren will be found in this position until they become partakers of the divine nature to a greater extent than ever they have been in the past....

"The rebuke of the Lord will rest upon those who would bar the way, that clearer light shall not come to the people. A great work is to be done, and God sees that our leading men have need of more light, that they may unite with the messengers whom He sends to accomplish the work that He designs shall be done. The Lord has raised up messengers, and endued them with His spirit, and has said, 'Cry aloud, spare not, lift up thy voice like a trumpet, and shew My people their transgression, and the house of Jacob their sins.' Let no one run the risk of interposing between the people and the message of Heaven. This message will go to the people; and if there were no voice among men to give it, the very stones would cry out."

"Organizations, institutions, unless kept by the power of God, will work under Satan's dictation to bring men under the control of men; and fraud and guile will bear the semblance of zeal and truth, and for the advancement of the kingdom of God...." —*Testimonies, Series B, No. 9, p. 24.*

"Laws and rules are being made at the centers of the work that will soon be broken into atoms. Men are not to dictate. It is not for those in places of authority to employ all their powers to sustain some, while others are cast down, ignored, forsaken, and left to perish. But it is the duty of the leaders to lend a helping hand to all who are in need. Let each work in the line God may indicate to him by His Holy Spirit....None are to exercise their human authority to bind the minds and souls of their fellow men. They are not to devise and put into practice methods and plans to bring every individual under their jurisdiction.

"Those who know the truth are to be worked by the Holy Spirit, and not themselves try to work the Spirit. If the cords are drawn much tighter, if the rules are made much finer, if men continue to bind their fellow laborers closer and closer to the commandments of men, many will be stirred by the Spirit of God to break every shackle, and assert their liberty in Christ Jesus." —*Review and Herald, July 23, 1895; The Church and Its Organization, p. 154.*

"The Lord will raise up men to bear the message of truth to the world and to His people. If those in responsible positions do not move onward in the opening providences of God, bearing an appropriate message for this time, the words of warning will be given to others who will be faithful to their trust. Even youthful Christians will be chosen to "cry aloud and spare not." —*Testimonies on S. S. Work, p. 56. Pub. in S. S. Worker, April 1892.*

"At present, I most decidedly dread to attend either campmeetings or Conferences. When present at such meetings, I am reigned up to speak plainly and strongly in regard to matters; for I dare not do otherwise than to tell the truth. The burden that comes upon me at such times is very heavy. The experiences I have passed through in attending meetings since returning to America have been most afflicting; for it seems as if my efforts are of none effect. The Testimonies borne bring upon me a great burden of soul, and seem to accomplish so little to change the order of things. The *Testimonies* are speculated upon, and do not reform existing evils.

"Just now my courage is not the best. Since the Fresno campmeeting, I have carried the burden of the Southern field in direct opposition to the plans of leading brethren. I have lost confidence in some of these men, as being taught and directed of God. If they are thus taught and directed I am not teaching the way of the Lord. Therefore, I am convinced that my place is at home. I can continue to write, if I avoid the crushing burdens that overwhelm me. And these burdens come upon me whenever I attend a meeting where there are men who I know are not walking in the counsel of God. I care not to face such matters any longer, for it seems useless. I long for retirement and mean to have it, if it be the Lord's will to give it to me." —*Mrs. E. G. White, in letter to Alonzo T. Jones, C. H. Jones, and M. C. Wilcox, January 27, 1903.*

"The light given by God for the people was hidden away in the publishing houses. The inner working of this matter was presented to me, and I saw that the very men who said that the canvassers would not handle my books were themselves arranging matters so they should not handle them. They told me falsehoods." —*Testimony to J. N. Loughborough, February 19, 1899.*

## The "Daily" and other Matters

The rejection of the divine purpose in health reform and to that extent at least of the Spirit of Prophecy, has a trail of evil consequences, the worst of which may not be manifest in the health of the rejectors. Many seem to think that their apparently robust physical condition is proof that the Spirit of God is wrong in the matter of health reform; but they are reaping another kind of results which they little suspect.

We might give an outline of the consequences as follows:

The rejection of the gospel of health as given by God through Inspiration to this people and movement, brings:

a.    First, guilt to the soul.

b.    A lessening of the distinctness of God's voice to the soul by His Spirit because the messages of His Spirit are not heeded; for two reasons: spirit and mind. He cannot enlighten the mind of a man who makes a cesspool of his stomach.

c.    Confusion in the Christian experience.

d.    Physical, mental, and spiritual injury.

These not only lead to spiritual backsliding but because of the lessening of the mental and spiritual perceptions and the consequent lessened measure of the spirit of God, such souls are easily led into error concerning many truths and many issues.

Having taken liberty with the messages of His Spirit along some lines, and having the spiritual vision dimmed, it is next easy and natural to take exceptoins to the messages of His Spirit on other points: and so men also question the writings of the Spirit of Prophecy on history, prophecy, dates, education, science, methods of labor, medical evangelism, etc., etc.

"Those who are in a position where it is possible to secure a vegetarian diet, but who choose to follow their own preferences in this matter, eating and drinking as they please, will gradually grow careless of the instruction the Lord has given regarding other phases of the present truth and will lose their perception of what is truth; they will surely reap as they have sown." —*Testimonies, Vol. 9, rip, 156, 157.*

While speaking of "dates" let it be noted that the point in the apostasy which God points out among us is not the question of the "Daily" upon which some people lay great stress. In a testimony given July 31, 1910, entitled, *Our Attitude Toward Doctrinal Controversy*, the following statements are made:

"I have had no instruction on the point under discussion." Then, regardless of the merits or errors of either side of that question, it is not a great testing question.

Again, "As this is not a test question, I entreat of my brethren that they shall not allow the enemy to triumph by having it treated as such. The work that the Lord has given us at this time is to present to the people the true light in regard to the testing questions of obedience and salvation—the commandments of God and the testimony of Jesus Christ."

The test, then, is not over the "Daily," nor can the apostasy be concerning it.

But the test and the apostasy always have been over obedience to God and loyalty to His living voice in the church, and these are the two things presented in this thesis.

"Obedience is the test of discipleship." —*Mount of Blessing, p. 210.*

As already stated, the great test in all ages has been obedience, and very often the crucial part of this test has been whether or not the people would obey or reject the messages sent from heaven for their day; and the sign of absolute loyalty and perfect obedience always has been the Sabbath. There will come a time when we will "proclaim the Sabbath more fully." This prophecy will be at least partially fulfilled when we teach that loyalty and obedience includes obedience to His laws of health. That this relation between the Sabbath and the medical missionary work does exist may be seen in the following quotation:

"Thus genuine medical missionary work is bound up inseparably with the keeping of God's command-ments, of which the Sabbath is especially mentioned, since it is the great memorial of God's creative work. Its observance is bound up with the work of restoring the moral image of God in man. This is the ministry which God's people are to carry forward at this time. This ministry, rightly performed, will bring rich blessings to the church." —*Testimonies, Vol. 6, p. 266.*

## *The General Condition of the SDA Church*

The statement made in all the preceding pages concerning the situation in the denomination seems unbelievably bad. It is so bad that a terrible risk is met in making such a statement; but the careful student of the Spirit of Prophecy is forced to this conclusion and is then forbidden to hold his peace.

That such is indeed the case, the indulgence of the reader is asked, and consideration is invited to the following statements on the general condition of our people. All of these statements were made several years ago and so would not even be adequate to correctly describe the conditions of the church today, because all admit that spirituality is steadily declining.

"I am filled with sadness when I think of our condi-tion as a people. The Lord has not closed heaven to us, but our own course of continual backsliding has separated us from God. Pride, covetousness, and love of the world have lived in the heart without fear of banishment or condemnation. Grievous and presumptuous sins have dwelt among us. And yet the general opinion is that the church is flourishing, and that peace and spiritual prosperity are in all her borders.

"The church has turned back from following Christ her Leader and is steadily retreating toward Egypt. Yet few are alarmed or astonished at their want of spiritual power. Doubt, and even disbelief of the testimonies of the Spirit of God, is leavening our churches everywhere." —*Testimonies, Vol. 5, p. 217.*

Note that the "general opinion" is on the wrong side, and does not recognize the true condition in the church.

"It is a solemn and terrible truth that many who have been zealous in proclaiming the third angel's message are now becoming listless and indifferent! The line of demarcation between worldlings and many professed Christians is almost indistinguishable. Many who once were earnest Adventists are conforming to the world—to its practices, its customs, its selfishness. Instead of leading the world to render obedience to God's law, the church is uniting more and more closely with the world in transgression. Daily the church is becoming converted to the world." —*Ibid., Vol. 8, pp. 118, 119.*

We look at Israel in her various experiences and say to ourselves: We would not have done as they did. But we would have! The following statements make it plain.

"There is a deplorable lack of spirituality among our people....For years I have felt deep anguish of soul as the Lord has presented before me the want in our churches of Jesus and His love....I have seen...that unless the pride of man should be abased and Christ exalted we should, as a people, be in no better condition to receive Christ at His second advent than were the Jewish people to receive Him at His first advent." —*Testimonies, Vol. 5, pp. 727, 728.*

"I was pointed back to ancient Israel. But two of the adults of the vast army that left Egypt entered the land of Canaan. Their dead bodies were strewn in the wilderness because of their transgressions. Modern Israel are in greater danger of forgetting God and being led into idolatry than were His ancient people." —*Ibid., Vol. 1, p. 609.*

"The same disobedience and failure which were seen in the Jewish church have characterized in a greater degree the people who have had this great light from heaven in the last messages of warning." —*Ibid., Vol. 5, p. 456.*

"As the storm approaches, a large class who have professed faith in the third angel's message, but have not been sanctified through obedience to the truth, abandon their position and join the ranks of the opposition." —*Great Controversy, p. 608.*

"Soon God's people will be tested by fiery trials, and the great proportion of those who now appear to be genuine and true will prove to be base metal....To stand in defense of truth and righteousness when the majority forsake us, to fight the battle of the Lord when champions are few—this will be our test. At this time we must gather warmth from the coldness of others, courage from their cowardice, and loyalty from their treason." —*Testimonies, Vol. 5, p. 136.*

"In the last vision given me, I was shown the startling fact that but a small portion of those who now profess the truth will be sanctified by it and be saved. Many will get above the simplicity of the work. They will conform to the world, cherish idols, and become spiritually dead. The humble, self sacrificing followers of Jesus will pass on to perfection, leaving behind the indifferent and lovers of the world." —*Testimonies, Vol. 1, p. 608.*

"...from what was shown me, but a small number of those now professing to believe the truth would eventually be saved—not because they could not be saved, but because they would not be saved in God's own appointed way. The way marked out by our divine Lord is too narrow and the gate too strait to admit them while grasping the world, or while cherishing selfishness or sin of any kind. There is no room for these things; and yet there are but few who will consent to part with them, that they may pass the narrow way and enter the strait gate." —*Ibid., Vol. 2, p. 445.*

Note a significant statement to the effect that heresies will come in and sift us as wheat.

"God will arouse His people; if other means fail, heresies will come in among them, which will sift them, separating the chaff from the wheat." —*Gospel Workers, p. 299.*

Let it here be noted that the General Conference statistical reports show that over 5000 people are disfellowshipped annually in the United States and Canada for apostasy.

Read carefully the chapters entitled: *The Seal of God, Testimonies*, Vol. 5, pp. 207-216; *The Testimony Slighted, Ibid.*, pp. 62-84; *The Laodicean Church, Ibid.*, Vol. 3, pp. 252-304.

To any believer in the Spirit of Prophecy these statements show that the condition of the church has not been painted darker in this thesis than it is. The sickness is upon us. If the diagnosis in these pages is wrong, let someone arise and give the correct diagnosis; but let him show it from the words of God.

# A Reformation

## Remedy —Christ Our Righteousness

A reformation of gigantic proportions is the greatest need of the hour, but it needs to be the kind for which God is calling, and not any kind of a substitute. It should be builded upon the acceptance of "the gospel in all its fullness." It should result in a thorough repentance of our "besetting sins" over the "stumbling blocks" of our denominational history; and such repentance should be followed by reformation and obedience. Any reformation or spiritual revival in our midst which ignores these (and there will be many) will be a false substitute and will be accompanied by a "power" full of danger.

A reformation or spiritual revival which leaves out the besetting sins dealt with in this thesis will descend to the level of the revival efforts of other Protestant churches and will be on the basis of accepting Christ in name while still failing to heed the definite messages He has these many years been sending to this people. Such an acceptance of Him by Seventh-day Adventists is a mockery to God.

Such revival efforts put forth by workers and leaders among us who have closed their eyes and ears these many years to the right appeals of the Spirit of Prophecy and ignored the place God has appointed for health reform in a spiritual revival will present a camouflaged acceptance of Christ without pointing out the definite sins which the real Christ is pointing out to the Laodicean church.

Let us have reformations based upon "the faith once delivered to the saints." Let us "make regular,

71

organized efforts to lift the church members out of the dead level in which they have been for years. Send out into the churches workers who will live the principles of health reform. Let those be sent who can see the necessity of self-denial in appetite, or they will be a snare to the church." —*Testimonies, Vol. 6, p. 267.*

"Send into the churches workers who will set the principles of health reform in their connection with the third angel's message, before every family and individual Encourage all to take a part in work for their fellowmen, and see if the breath of life will not quickly return to these churches." —*Special Testimonies to Ministers and Workers, No. 11, p. 19.*

## The Medical Work

As has already been stated, the elements needed to inspire a sound Christian experience in place of the false one described in these pages is reposed in the gospel of health which has been intrusted in a special sense to our medical workers. Although God says: "The medical missionary work is sick, and needs the restoring power of the great Healer, before it can accomplish a work in harmony with its name" (*Testimonies, Series B, No. 2, p. 24*). Yet the health message still has the "key" to the situation, and, in a certain sense, the use of it is committed largely to the hands of the medical workers, in that God would have them to stand as champions of the message that can save the day for the denomination. This helps us to understand why God says, "If you are a Christian and a competent physician, you are qualified to do tenfold more good as a missionary for God than if you were to go forth merely as a preacher of the word." —*Healthful Living, par. 1133.*

It is a very significant fact that, when the time for transition in denominational officers arrived, and the crowning efforts of the twenty-one-year administration was made for the latter rain and failed, at that identical time there should come a unifying spirit among the health workers assembled at the Conference; that they should teach a more correct view of Christian experience than was taught in the evangelical sections of the Conference; that they should rally more fully than for many years to the spiritual significance of the health work; and that they should lay definite and far-reaching plans to restore to the denomination the "lost art" of the "right arm" of the message.

This time of readjustment in the organization is heaven's opportunity to once more bring these matters to the attention of the leaders of this people and, if possible, reach the ears of the people with the "gospel in all its fullness" and set before them a balanced Christian experience, a balanced message, and balanced methods of labor in presenting the gospel to the world and to our churches.

The possibilities before our medical workers at this time are almost beyond conception, if they will place themselves at God's disposal. These possibilities constitute such a mighty call to consecration to the task as has seldom, if ever, been witnessed in the history of the world; for the crowning work of all the ages is to be done now; the long controversy is to be finished. God on the one side has been saying that men should obey Him. Satan has said they should not, and cannot do so; and the vast majority of human witnesses have been on the wrong side. God's work in the earth cannot close—the controversy cannot be settled—unless a *church* demonstrates that God is right, and this can be demonstrated only by coming to perfect obedience. Therefore, God waits now, not for one or two men, or a few men, to actually achieve victory, but He waits for His *church* to do it. This cannot be done without the gospel of health, without obedience to natural law as a branch out of the moral law. This is why the health work is so important, and this is why the enemy battles the health work harder than any other work we try to do.

But to meet such a tremendous issue and to carry such a responsibility our medical folks must bestir themselves and shake off shackles which have long bound them, and inaugurate a thorough reformation in their midst. They must remember that God has spoken to them as much cutting reproof as He has to the evangelical workers; that He demands of them a housecleaning; that they have left the road on the opposite side from their brethren in that they have been lacking in spiritual things and have been overmaterialistic while their brethren have been spiritualizing away certain things which God wanted to remain material things; that while their evangelical brethren have been quibbling over the Spirit of Prophecy they too have done the same thing (each side claiming to be guiltless in this matter, but both alike guilty), till they put the science of the world above the voice of Inspiration in various medical questions (such as the use of drugs in place of God's remedies), where God would test their faith in Him; that, whereas a besetting sin with the preachers has been indulgence of appetite, a besetting sin of the doctors has been the use of drugs; that they have put the requirements of the world concerning medical education above the instructions of God so that the much study of the "maxims of the Scribes and Pharisees" crowds out the study of the words of God and

His remedies, and physiology from the divine standpoint.

We spend so much time studying the things we profess not to believe in order to secure a right to practice the things we profess to believe, that when we get through we have become so inoculated with the error that we just naturally go out and do that which we studied so much, and the things we started out to do are lost to our view if they indeed ever were clear in our minds.

## Medical Schools

Through the following quotations the reader will see how God looks upon all the medical schools in the world:

"Not one of the schools of medicine so highly lauded in the world is approved in the courts above, nor do they bear the heavenly superscription and endorsement. You are not justified in advocating one school above another, as though it was the only one worthy of respect. Those who vindicate one school of medicine and bitterly condemn another are actuated by a zeal that is not according to knowledge. With what Pharisaic pride some men look down upon others who have not received a diploma from the so-called standard school! All this proves that they cannot see afar off, and have not been purged from their old sins. They need to humble themselves at the cross of Calvary. This spirit will never be acknowledged in heaven, nor will men that cherish it ever hear the "Well done." I have spoken plainly in regard to your feelings concerning the methods of practice. Some of you have been as zealous in exalting what your school advocated as though the Lord has specified that very method was the only one to be allowed. The use of drugs has resulted in far more harm than good, and, should our physicians who claim to believe the truth almost entirely dispense with medicine and faithfully practice along the lines of hygiene, using nature's remedies, far greater success would attend their efforts. There is no need whatever to exalt the method whereby drugs are administered. I know whereof I speak. Brethren in the medical profession, I entreat you to think candidly and put away childish things. The Lord is not pleased with our attitude toward those who have graduated in what you call inferior schools. He does not approve of the spirit that actuates you. God will judge as by what we ought to have been, what we ought to have done, had we been obedient children. We cannot escape the consequence of our omissions and mistakes even though we cannot see them or estimate their results....

"Feeling existed in regard to the method that was used at the _____, under Dr. _____, director. Dr. _____ with the utmost confidence and assurance extolled the 'regular' practice, depreciated the practice of 'homeopathy,' and made the most extravagant statements in regard to the regular practice. Some might take these statements as verity and truth, but I know that they are not correct; for the practice of both systems and their results have been laid open before me, and I know that the statements he made were not correct. But this is due to the narrow cut of the man. The system in which he has been educated he regards as the best of all others. The Lord regards all this talk as He regards the talk of the Pharisees—as the invention and traditions of men. All who receive their education from a 'regular' school and are molded by the spirit of the educators, generally act out the impressions they have received from instructors, and denounce every other system as Satanic. Is this the way of the Lord?...The use of drugs in our institutions, to the extent that they are used, is a libel upon the name of 'hygienic institutions' for the treatment of the sick. The physician needs to be converted on this point as decidedly as the sinner needs the converting power of God on his life and character in order to become a pure-hearted Christian. Let the students who go to receive a medical education at the medical institutions of our land learn all they possibly can of the principles of life, but let them discard error and not become bigots. I should not speak thus plainly unless I felt that it was necessary." —*From Dr. David Poulson's private collection.* Who is making a serious study to find out what use can be made of less poisonous herbs, as suggested in the messages sent to our institutions? What does dietetics amount to in our institutions? What about the outdoor labor for patients and for students? Who is studying and trying to find the best methods of treating diseases like malaria, syphilis, yaws and other tropical diseases, without the use of drugs that we know are dangerous and often cause damage? Are we trying to lead people at home and in the foreign field away from an "educated" type of witchcraft, where people are taught to look for the "spectacular" in some drug rather than to simple methods that have the evident blessing of God? Are we teaching people to look to a cleaner, more enlightened "witch" with his "potions," or are we teaching them to look to the One Who can complete the healing of both body and soul?

A few medical men in various parts of the country are succeeding with malaria and other diseases which are supposed to have no other remedy than certain "specific" drug treatment. This is despite the fact that these "specific" remedies have proven hopelessly inadequate. The fear of being classed as unorthodox seems to prevent Loma Linda from even testing some of the remedies suggested by these men even though these remedies are more in harmony with the methods we should be using and less harmful than present drug therapy.

The spirit of reform does not run as high in our medical work today as it did years ago when Doctor Kellogg was willing to receive the *Testimonies* sent to him.

We are far ahead of the world in the possession of light on all these questions because we have for years been possessors of light from heaven, but some in the world are actually making better use of the glimmerings of light they have and the little bit they get from our books, or contact with our workers, than we are of our flood of light; and it is so much so that they are putting us to shame, and we have, by our unbelief, made ourselves the "tail" and have become their students rather than their educators as God set us in the world to be. We are seeking recognition from the very people to whom God sent us to be instructors. Note the following:

"Be on guard as physicians. You can serve the Lord in your position by working with new methods and discarding drugs. As reformers we are to reform the medical practice by educating toward the light. Our work is to be done in the full recognition of God." —*Special Testimonies, MSS 63-99.*

"Study the Bible more and the theories of the medical fraternity less, and you will have greater spiritual health. Your mind will be clearer and more vigorous. Much that is embraced in the medical course is positively unnecessary. Those who take a medical training spend a great deal of time in learning that which is merely rubbish. Many of the theories they learn may be compared in value to the traditions and maxims taught by the Scribes and Pharisees. Many of the intricacies with which they have to become familiar are an injury to their minds." —*Words of Counsel, a leaflet published at St. Helena, California, October 16, 1903; and Loma Linda Messages, p. 190.*

Our affiliation with the medical world in seeking after their recognition upon their basis is giving the glory and honor that belongs to the God of Israel over to the god Ekron and worshipping at his shrine. And, furthermore, this contact and association with and catering to the world in our medical education is like the vortex of a whirlpool exerting a mighty suction on our entire educational system tending to drag it all down into the world.

If we took the same spineless attitude toward religious liberty that we do toward medical liberty, we would be a laughingstock even to ourselves.

There are examples of this kind of thing in the world that put us to shame and which we would do well to emulate.

Priessnitz, called "the father of hydrotherapy," had a hard time with the medical profession, which apparently dominated state law then somewhat as it does now. At one time persecution by the medical profession waxed so fierce that Priessnitz was tried and sentenced, in 1829; but the sentence was revoked on appeal to a higher court, and in 1831 he was granted official permission to conduct a hydropathic establishment. In 1838 the Imperial Home Office at Vienna sent Baron Turkheim, a man of scientific education and high culture, as well as a court Councillor, to Graefenberg, to investigate the disturbing reports about Priessnitz. After spending some time observing the methods and effects of the Water Cure, talking with Priessnitz and with his patients, also conferring with persons in the neighborhood, the Baron carried back to Vienna the word that "nobody was less a quack or an impostor than the water doctor of Graefenberg." Whereupon the Imperial Austrian Government issued an order, in 1838, authorizing Priessnitz to "have the same privileges as members of the medical profession in the practice of hygienic remedies." He did not win his needed recognition (the privilege to work) by studying or catering to the things he professed not to believe.

Osteopaths and chiropractors set us an example in persistency. After permission to practice the methods to which they hold had been denied they continued to press for recognition and received it. If we had been as persistent as they, and stuck to our light and message as they have to their theories, we would have had, long ago, all the recognition we needed, for God promised it to us.

"The education that meets the world's standard is to be less and less valued by those who are seeking for efficiency in carrying the medical missionary work in connection with the work of the third angel's message. They are to be educated from the standpoint of conscience, and, as they conscientiously and faithfully follow right methods in their treatment of the sick, these methods will come to be recognized as preferable to the methods to which many have become accustomed, which demand the use of poisonous drugs." —*Testimonies, Vol. 9, p. 175.*

## Gideon and the Heathen

The following quotation from Doctor Mary McReynolds is quite to the point.

"Do you know I have thought much of late of Gideon and his experience? You know God gave him very definite experience and instruction. He selected his coworkers; He gave him every sign he asked for; and then the promise of Judges 7:7 and the command 'Arise' —Go (us. 9). Then, reading the unbelief still in that man's heart, God gave him an experience that should warn us —and put us to shame if we hesitate and make it necessary again at this late hour in our experience: 'But, if thou fear...thou shalt hear what they [the heathen host] say;...And it was so,...' —*Judges 7:10, 11, 15*. After Gideon heard the heathen's 'interpretation' of God's plan, he 'worshiped' and claimed the victory God had promised (vss. 7, 9) and led his men out to accomplish the work.

"Now the history of our medical work runs quite parallel with this experience.

"Prior to 1865, light on health reform was given which our people disregarded (*Testimonies, Vol. 1, p, 485*). In 1865 appeared the book *How to Live*, in which are five chapters of strong instruction. Here at the same time *Facts of Faith* was printed, the last chapter of which is on 'health' and contains some remarkable statements. In *Testimonies* Vol. 1, p. 489, also, appears the first call for sanitarium work. Then followed, through the years, the definite instruction in regard to methods to be used in this work.

"As early as *Testimonies*, Vol. 1, p. 640, came the first instruction in regard to occupational therapy, especially outdoor work. This, you may recall, was the only part of our therapy which was given directly to us by inspiration. The matter of hydrotherapy was amplified upon by the Spirit of Phophecy, but was first practiced by other physicians in the East—'Let the feeble ones be led out, as they can bear it, to cultivate the beautifully situated acres owned by the Institute....Let their labor be a part of their prescription, as much as the taking of baths.'

"It is interesting to note that the Lord emphasized this same line of work when He began to build up another medical college which was to accomplish what Battle Creek failed to accomplish. 'By outdoor exercises and working in the soil men and women will regain their health. Rational methods for the cure of disease will be used in a variety of ways. Drugs will be discarded.' (*Loma Linda Messages, p. 6, July 1905.*) And by the way, I am still praying for the fulfillment of that which to me is a precious promise, that the time will come on Loma Linda Hill when medicines which contain poisonous properties will no longer be administered to the human bodies entrusted to our care as physicians and nurses.

"Now I want to take up the line of thought which I left a paragraph or two back, that just as God gave Gideon definite instruction, so He gave us definite instruction for our medical practice many, many years ago and repeated it again in the early part of the 1900's, and still there was so much doubt and so much hesitancy that He has permitted us to repeat Gideon's experience.

"Charles P. Emerson, Chairman of the *Committee on Equipment for Teaching Hospitals*, as reported in the proceedings of the 29th annual meeting of the A. M. A., Chicago, 1919, p. 30:

"We are unworthy heirs of the Greek inheritance since we have abandoned the gymnastics, hydrotherapy, and other forms of physiatrics which formed so important a part of their therapy. The heavy hand of the Arabian is indeed still upon us, and, thanks to the education of our fathers, the patient still expects the doctor to prescribe some medicine, and more the better. Many doctors still feel that it is beneath their dignity to treat a case other than by advice and a prescription. And yet in the majority of cases non-medical therapy is actually of greater importance than drugs. The result is that dietetics, hydrotherapy, electrotherapy, thermotherapy, etc., etc., are abandoned measures in combating disease; each is the valuable and efficient weapon of a school of irregulars, and we are ashamed to use them. How much of these does a teaching hospital practice in the average curriculum of pharmacology and materia medica?

"The medical schools should lead in a radical reform in medical practice by teaching all that is good in each and every form of therapy. This would take time and equipment and teachers. The teaching hospital should have a diet laboratory, a real solarium, and rooms for other forms of such therapy. This equipment would take space, but the apparatus itself would not be expensive.'

"Dr. Ray Lyman Wilbur, president of Stanford University, told the American Medical Association today (March 6, 1922) that medical education was 'such a stagnant mess that the student emerged a mystified doctor.'"

Satan throws dust in the eyes of our medical workers and leads them into commercialism, professionalism, overmuch surgery, worldly science, public health work, humanitarianism, or knocking other cults when we should be building one of our own instead—anything and everything to occupy our attention so long as we do not have a clear vision and do not give ourselves entirely to our only God-given work, bearing a message for the saving of souls, our own included.

A message is not proclaimed primarily with a knife, with medicine, or even with treatment; but by instruction. There is a way by which and an extent to which these may aid in imparting instruction for the saving of the soul, if used according to the word of God rather than contrary to that work; but, to accomplish this, all these things ought to make us more expert and efficient in imparting the spiritual message rather than less so (and the latter has become proverbial and a byword among us).

There is a great lesson in 2 Samuel 18:19-32 for our medical folks at this time. Ahimaaz insisted that he should run and bear tidings to the king. "And he said, All is well." But he had no tidings though he insisted that he must run. He knew something was going on and that there ought to be something to tell, but the vital thing he did not know, and so had no message. The king said, "Turn aside and stand here, and he turned aside and stood still." After him came the Cushite who had the tidings and bore the message. The time must come when our medical folks who have insisted on "running" but have not been bearers of "tidings" are to stand aside and give place to those who have the message and whose first business is to proclaim it and who make their scientific training and acquired skill a means of more scientifically and skillfully telling the message.

The world teaches medical science in an imperfect way for the sake of health. While this is a worthy work, yet the commission given to Seventh-day Adventist physicians is a much higher calling, it being to help prepare a people for the coming of the Lord. When we teach medical science according to the wisdom and word of God it has character as its object, and eternity as its goal. We should make that our first work, and regard our medical training as merely adjunctive to that.

Merely to find employment within the organization is not sufficient. Were every medical student we graduate to find employment within the organization, to go out and do the same sort of medical work done by the majority in the past, that would not change the situation, but would only enlarge and aggravate the present condition. We must do more than that. We must set our hearts on remedying these conditions and helping mightily to prepare this people for translation.

This has a large bearing on the sort of training to be given medical students and nurses. Students should be taught that no science is worth anything to a Seventh-day Adventist only as it is an integral part of the science of saving souls.

## No Substitute for Reform

This same thing applies to the Medical Missionary extension work to be undertaken from this time on. If the extension medical work is to be largely hospital, surgical, or dispensary work, Satan will triumph again. We need to get the thought born within us that there is no substitute for reform and that when we get our eyes off that, it is a trick of the devil to detract our attention from the vital thing which God has waited these many years for us to do, and still waits. It is possible that science has in many ways become such a substitute for reform. If it should be proven that appendicitis, as an example for instance, is caused by wrong habits of living, then it would be that to cut that out and tell the patient we had cured him would be to have taken out an accumulated result of his bad habits and left his bad habits —made surgery a substitute for reform,

The same might be true of legitimate treatments, of gland products, or colon treatment, etc., etc.; the principle is a broad one.

"The Lord desires, through His people, to answer Satan's charges by showing the result of obedience to right principles. He desires our health institutions to stand as witness for truth. They are to give character to the work which must be carried forward in these last days in restoring man through a reformation of the habits, appetites, and passions. Seventh-day Adventists are to be represented to the world by the advanced principles of health reform which God has given us." —MSS "God's Design in Establishing Sanitariums," Dec. 22, 1899.

We are to get hard after the "habits, appetites and passions," and there can be no substitute for this work. Do we make it plain? Our work of restoration is through reformation. That is our great work, and we are doing but very little of it because we are copying so much after the world.

Our medical work is to be different from any other medical work in the world. Many act as if they did not believe that, for we constantly go to the world to learn from them and copy them as closely as possible. That makes us "orthodox!"

The medical work we ought to do springs from the bosom of the message more than from science. Therefore no one in the world could do the medical work we ought to do unless he had the same message.

There are others working in reform lines and doing better in some aspects, with the little light they have, than we are, with our much light. They all go hopelessly astray at some point because of a lack of light. We should be able to show evolutionists, atheists, agnostics, theosophists, etc. a better way than the road they are groping along, but too often they put us to shame.

God has committed a specific work to us different from any other medical work in the world.

### *Appeal to Medical Workers*

The question of the hour is —Will the medical folks abandon their unbelief and apostasy on the right-hand side of the road and return to the middle of it; and will the evangelical folks (with all the rest) abandon their unbelief and apostasy and return to the middle of the road, and all join together on the divine platform of the "faith once delivered to the saints?"

Who will "come up to the help of the Lord against the mighty?" Those who unite on this platform, from both the evangelical and medical sides of the working forces, will be used of God in the finishing of the work, but those who refuse to do so will sooner or later drop out by the way like the Israelites in the wilderness. Let it not be said of the reader that his "house is left unto you desolate" because "ye would not."

We invite you to view the complete
selection of titles we publish at:
**www.TEACHServices.com**

scan with your mobile
device to go directly
to our website

Please write or email us your praises, reactions, or
thoughts about this or any other book we publish at:

# TEACH Services, Inc.
## P U B L I S H I N G
www.TEACHServices.com ● (800) 367-1844

**Info@TEACHServices.com**

TEACH Services, Inc., titles may be purchased in bulk
for educational, business, fund-raising, or sales
promotional use. For information, please e-mail:

**BulkSales@TEACHServices.com**

Finally if you are interested in seeing
your own book in print, please contact us at

**publishing@TEACHServices.com**

We would be happy to review your manuscript for free.

www.ingramcontent.com/pod-product-compliance
Lightning Source LLC
Chambersburg PA
CBHW060440090426
42733CB00011B/2346